THE SOUND
THAT CHANGED
EVERYTHING

A Prophetic Call to the Purposes of God
(and how you can hear it)

THE SOUND
THAT CHANGED
EVERYTHING

A Prophetic Call to the Purposes of God
(and how you can hear it)

STEPHEN EVERETT

Treasure House

An Imprint of
Destiny Image® Publishers, Inc.
P.O. Box 310
Shippensburg, PA 17257-0310

"For where your treasure is, there will your heart be also."
Matthew 6:21

ISBN 0-7684-3011-9

For Worldwide Distribution
Printed in the U.S.A.

This book and all other Destiny Image, Revival Press, MercyPlace,
Fresh Bread, Destiny Image Fiction, and Treasure House books
are available at Christian bookstores and distributors worldwide.

For a U.S. bookstore nearest you, call 1-800-722-6774.
For more information on foreign distributors, call 717-532-3040.
Or reach us on the Internet:
www.destinyimage.com

DEDICATION

Dedicated to all those who recognize the need for change in the Body of Christ, unity, and spiritual relevance. Our hour has come.

ACKNOWLEDGMENTS

To my wife, Ann, for her approbation and for tirelessly assisting me by editing this manuscript.

To my colleagues, Apostles Carl C. Alexander and William Hinn, for their encouragement during this project. We have ministered many times together. Our networking efforts will be beneficial to the cause of Christ now and in the future.

To the Holy Spirit, my Teacher, who unlocked the principles I share in this manuscript.

CONTENTS

PREFACE

The new millennium has commenced. We are one of two generations that have witnessed the beginning of a new millennium since the New Covenant started. Surprisingly to some Christians, the Church is still on planet Earth. We are just beginning to rise out of a theological thicket—a maze of inaccurate ideas. Where do we go from here? Is there a new sound cascading in all the Earth?

For some time I have desired to write a book about the current global reformation of the Church. The annual convention at Grace Immanuel Bible Church in Detroit, Michigan, gave me the inspiration I needed. What is written is the direct product of years of meditations and gleanings, as God would speak to me personally and through others.

I have come to appreciate more fully the message of the Gospel. The Gospel is a story of reformation—God repositioning fallen mankind in Christ. Although the Authorized Bible only uses the word *reformation* once (Heb. 9:10), it conceptualizes its operation in both testaments. Every place the Gospel has been embraced people have advanced. Contrast this with the nations that have been besieged by other gods and philosophies, including supposedly atheistic nations. Their progress has been slow and minimal.

The Protestant Reformation produced vast improvements in most Western European cultures. Europe was known as the "first world" to many of the first American settlers, therefore being a center of fundamental Bible revelation and world missions. After persecuted separatists moved across the Atlantic Ocean and colonized the Americas, we have witnessed the gradual rise of the United States to become a superpower. North America was called the "second world," becoming a center of Pentecostal revelation and missions.

Now we have come to the third season of reformation. God's movements are no longer polarized in Europe or North America. Countries known as the "third world," or developing nations in South America, Africa, and Asia, are now centers of profound Kingdom advancement. The Southern Hemisphere has awakened to a brand-new day! God is doing a new thing; it's a new feast, and a shift has happened in the Heavens again.

There is a distinct, joyful sound from the Heavens vibrating in the Earth again. The Scripture says, "Blessed (happy, fortunate, to be envied) are the people who know the joyful sound (who understand and appreciate the spiritual blessings symbolized by the feasts); they walk, O Lord, in the light and favor of Your countenance!" (Ps. 89:15 AMP) It is not the rehearsed sounds of the Feasts of Passover and Pentecost only, but the distinguished sound of the Feast of Tabernacles. This sound is arising in the midst of many sounds. The apostle Paul stated eloquently, "For if the trumpet makes an uncertain sound, who will prepare for battle?" (1 Cor. 14:8) For reasons known only to Him, God has allowed certain prophetic voices to clearly articulate His wonderful heart in these days.

I find that other legitimate prophetic people have no clue about the ramifications of the Feast of Tabernacles. Moreover, others are speaking by the spirit of speculation and uncertainty. Human beings generally speak out of the context of whatever end-time philosophy they embrace. Ideas are being suggested as truths that are no more than folly and the peddling of fear. What is truly understood by some scholars is never mentioned in the average pulpit. Because of our responsibility to speak forth the purposes of God, we must be sure that our voices are distinct notes of what God is saying in these times. Two questions must be asked: 1) "What time is it in the economy of God?" and 2) "Is it time for a new feast of the Lord?" Without hesitation, I concur with many other credible men and women of God that it is time for another feast of the Lord in the Church, and the time is now!

History reveals that every generation thinks that theirs is the one that will usher in the return of the Lord Jesus back to the Earth. It is clear that up to this time each was considerably off target in their calculations. The Scripture once again is very clear on this matter: those times and seasons are in the hands of the heavenly Father. Our present job description is to occupy the Earth until Christ comes and prepare a generation to advance the Kingdom of God to the next level.

After Adam's failure in the Garden of Eden, God personally taught Adam about the next level of operation in the Kingdom. Adam was responsible to teach his sons Cain and Abel the things he had learned. Abel caught it and Cain did not. Cain finally murdered Abel, successfully killing the one who represented the new thing in the Earth at the time. God raised up Seth in Abel's stead because His purpose must march on like a mighty army. We must instruct and prepare our sons for the next level in God, not kill them with lifeless traditions and ambiguity. Mature men and women of God are the guardians and custodians of the Kingdom mysteries, as God imparts new impetus into the womb of this generation.

The initial descendants of Adam were terminated in the days of Noah and the massive Flood. Noah and his family were left to inherit the earth. They were given the same assignment as the first man and woman. All the descendants of Noah's sons have run the gamut of world history without executing the full change God intended. Six days have expired and each group that has been the dominant group has proven as carnal as the previous one. Thoughts of superiority to other men spoiled the opportunity to serve them. At first it was Ham's seed dominating, then Shem's seed, and finally the sons of Japheth. God is now raising up a new

13

species of mankind globally. This season in God is for whosoever will, let them come.

I foresee a generation coming, no matter the chronological age, which will package into one expression all we have ever dreamed of. It is to them that this book is primarily addressed. Peter said, "Receiving the end of your faith, even the salvation of your souls. Of which salvation the prophets have inquired and searched diligently, who prophesied of the grace that should come unto you" (1 Pet. 1:9-10 KJV). The Old Testament prophets spoke with timely candor but had no idea they were speaking to us until the Holy Spirit revealed it to them. We are currently speaking forth the things of God and at the same time prophesying to generations to come. It would behoove us to understand that fact.

This book and others like it will render a very important service to the generational purposes of God. They will serve as a legacy of truth. In the middle of this century, the children of God will be able to look back and slightly perceive how some of us were thinking as God launched this all-important third millennium A.D. This is the *third day* or *millennium* from Jesus and the *seventh millennium* from Adam. This concept is derived from Second Peter 3:8 and Psalm 90:4: "But, beloved, be not ignorant of this one thing, that one day is with the Lord as a thousand years, and a thousand years as one day" (2 Pet. 3:8 KJV). God built Himself a man for the seventh day at the close of the sixth day. (See Genesis 1:26-28.) Once again God was building Himself a corporate man at the end of the twentieth century, which concluded the sixth millennium from Adam.

As a young Christian I read books that mentored my understanding in the things of God. It blessed me to see how God moved in the Welsh Revival, Azusa Street, the Latter Rain Movement, and other moves of God. I understood the twentieth century started with a bang through neo-Pentecostal experiences. God was also doing many wonderful things among our fundamentalist brethren. About every ten to twenty years He would add another line to what was already accomplished. It was interesting to see the pace escalate in the things God added to the Church as we have come to the twenty-first century.

In the future some inquiring, thirsty child of God will read about our day as I read about those days. Brethren in the 1990s have stated very well our hunger and need for renewal. We nodded our heads and said, "Yes! You're right! We're hungry! What's next?" This book addresses some of what is next for the Body of Christ. I trust this book will stand as a bulwark of truth battling against the false gods and philosophies of this age and every thought that speaks incorrectly to God's purposes. Many sounds are being made. All of them are significant but not necessarily correct. May the Lord open our ears to hear, our eyes to see, and our hearts to perceive. May we come to know the sound in the Earth that is changing everything.

—Stephen Everett

FOREWORD

The Scriptures declare plainly: "It is the glory of God to conceal a thing, but the honor of kings to search out the matter." As I walk with Apostle Stephen Everett in friendship and ministry, I believe among the many wonderful expressions of his personality and giftings is his tenure as a Kingdom father. This emerges with pristine clarity and authority both before God and men. In this book, *The Sound That Changed Everything*, it is clear Steve has again drawn from the fountains of God's vast wisdom and has delivered with authenticity something of God's voice.

Among other factors, two elements, which are critical evidence of the time of reformation or change, are the appearance of the reformer himself/herself and his/her message. These two serve as agents of change and remain as catalysts until the process comes to maturation.

The reformer Mohandas K. Gandhi said, "Mankind is notoriously too dense to read the signs that God sends them from time to time. We require drums to be beaten into our ears before we would wake from our trance and hear the warning."

Steve, like Jeremiah, heeded God's summons to the potter's house and saw God work the potter's wheels. He witnessed the manufacture of a vessel, the destruction of that same vessel, then the restoration of that vessel according to the potter's design and intent.

In 1967 Dr. Martin Luther King Jr., who was one of this century's greatest reformers, challenged the Church's then silent clergy "in a call to conscience" to speak out against what he regarded as an unjust war that was being fought in Vietnam. He then identified three prevailing evils in our society and declared, "Cowardice asks: Is it safe? Expediency asks: Is it political? Vanity asks: Is it popular?" But Conscience asks: "Is it right?"

If the Church must change, then the prophets of cowardice, expediency, and vanity must be bound to silence and irrelevance and let Conscience speak. You'll concur with me after reading this excellent work that my brother Stephen Everett is a voice of conscience for our present day Church.

—Carl C. Alexander, Apostle

FOREWORD

Throughout the generations when the Earth becomes void and darkness is upon the face of its deep, God calls light out of darkness. When drought has become the condition of man's heart and numbness his state, God makes a way in the wilderness and rivers in the desert. He decrees a trumpet sound in the midst of silence that resonates life, commanding change into the next generation.

A clear, clarion cry has been issued out of Heaven calling for a new spiritual generation that will expand the parameters of revelation. As an ambassador, Apostle Stephen Everett has clothed this sound with words that will reach deep down into the submerged chaos of the human condition, calling it to the cross of change and rightful inheritance.

The Master has aggressively tuned His servant, stretching the cords of his being and producing a well-balanced and distinct sound that harmonizes with Heaven. Now emerging out of obscurity, this reformer is paving a way for a new kind of believer, whose culture exemplifies the standards of the Kingdom.

Over the years I have always said that if I were to shine a light through Stephen Everett, it would appear the same on the other side, nothing in the way of the light of God. I consider it a privilege to be called his friend. To all with an ear to hear, herein is a *sound that will change everything*.

—William D. Hinn, Apostle

INTRODUCTION

*Behold, the former things have come to pass, and
new things I declare; before they spring forth I tell you
of them.* Isaiah 42:9

*Do not remember the former things, nor consider
the things of old.*
*Behold, I will do a new thing, now it shall spring
forth; shall you not know it? I will even make a road in
the wilderness and rivers in the desert.*
Isaiah 43:18-19

NEW THINGS

I have good news for all fundamental, Bible-believing
Christians: God does not change! (See John 8:58; Hebrews
13:8.) In Malachi 3:6a, the Lord said: "For I am the Lord, I do
not change!" God cannot be duplicated, altered, disguised,
perverted, or repeated. He cannot be transmuted—that is,
changed from His nature, form, substance, or state into
another. He is self-existent, self-sufficient, self-containing,
totally integrated, perfect, immutable, infinite, and timeless.[1]

As consistent as these truths are throughout every age,
God still does new things in the Earth with each succeeding
generation of mankind. Isaiah 43 deals with the new things
connected with Israel's deliverance out of Egyptian bondage.
The creation account of Genesis 1 demonstrates God's ability to do new things every single day. A whirlwind glance of
the past millennium—all its highlights, achievements, and
discoveries—reveals the significance of new things in God's

interplay with human history. Although such a laundry list of highlights is not feasible for this book, it is important to look at some of the new things that have been discovered in the last few years, particularly in the advancement of computer technology.

In June 2001, Intel Corporation researchers, led by Dr. Robert Chau, announced that they had created the technology needed to produce the world's smallest and fastest silicon transistor on a mass scale. Tiny transistors such as these are just 20 nanometers long (a nanometer is one-billionth of a meter, or about 1/50,000th of a human hair) and 80 atoms wide. With these diminutive gatekeepers of electronic current, switching on and off 1.5 trillion times a second, microprocessors could complete a billion calculations in the time that it takes a person to blink. These transistors run at speeds of nearly 20 gigahertz, and just one year ago the top speed of a transistor was 1 gigahertz, which was considered absolutely breathtaking. Ultimately these tiny transistors will be placed in computers in the future.[2] This will make computer technology as we know it today obsolete.

This is a marvelous discovery! Nevertheless, it is all relative, for by the time technology is presented to the public, someone has already discovered something newer and more exciting! What was astounding, cutting-edge knowledge is now outmoded.

None of these discoveries would have been possible ten years ago because it was not the right season. God chooses specific seasons to reveal certain things. Our Father has opened the realm of the Spirit, and everything pertaining to life is within the parameter of the Spirit. There is a rent veil of knowledge and information never before available to mankind. Daniel said, "Many shall run to and fro, and knowledge shall be increased" (Dan. 12:4b KJV). By law most everything aligns to a pattern of generational advancement, except for the Church, which remains philosophically and operationally in a sort of "flat Earth society" paradigm.

We must be open to new things! The lightning speed by which they are being revealed is mind-boggling. Trends and pace of the past are far spent. This is the reason we declare without apology that God is doing a new thing in the Church. Either the Church will move with God in transition, or it will remain stagnant in what was once vanguard and cutting-edge. Just imagine using a computer chip of the 1980s with today's technology; or even worse, imagine using 1960s technology that controlled moon missions.

TRANSITION

With or without our permission, God is changing us! Change is an irrefutable constant in God's dealings with mankind. Since the turn of the millennium, the Church has gone through and continues to go through major transition. Precious men and women of God have sought to identify and explain the transition, knowing a new era has dawned upon the Earth. Sincere prophets, without speculation, are calling it everything from revival to reformation. Webster defines *transition* as "a passing from one condition, form, stage, activity, place, etc. to another."[3]

As with Jacob, God is wrestling each of us with the intent of winning. Our churchy activities, programs, and ideas are losing. If the truth were told, most of them are exacerbating us, if we are hungry for a greater manifestation of God and tired of hype. Operationally, we are transferring from a low-water mark in the Spirit to a higher calling. Paul, the apostle, encouraged us to "Set your mind on things above, not on things on the earth" (Col. 3:2).

The purpose of change is to purify the Body of Christ until we all come into the unity of the faith and are conformed into the image of Christ. Unity is not some idealism that creates uniformity; it is the Body of Christ finally appreciating and valuing all the parts and recognizing their contribution to the whole. The Lord created the unity of His Body and we can only keep it. *Conformed* means "jointly formed or similar."[4] I understand Christ is God's image and form. As the Church we have borne many other images and forms; however, we are yet to fully bear Christ maturely. Transition is a process, not an event, which removes us from where we are to God's goal. The ultimate achievement of transition is to come into the new thing God is currently doing.

I am writing this book as a statement of agreement with God's doings. Many of my colleagues and friends have encouraged me in this project. My first book, *The Mystery of Melchisedec*,[5] taught me several valuable and indispensable lessons. As the writer of the Book of the Hebrews says, "Therefore we must give the more earnest heed to the things we have heard, lest we drift away" (Heb. 2:1). When we allow pertinent lessons to drift or slip, it is equivalent to forsaking wisdom, knowledge, and understanding. (See Proverbs 3:19-21.) Perhaps in attempting to evaluate these lessons, the following short list emerges. Words such as *communication*, *timing*, and *audience* summarize my prolonged appraisal. Allow me, for a moment, to briefly examine each one.

COMMUNICATION

First of all, God is doing a *new thing* in the Earth. This is certainly not an improved form of the old, inadequate things of previous seasons. If this were the case, two thousand years ago God would have improved the old man rather than totally discarding him. The Father's children need prophetic teachings that are clearly communicated and articulate the change. *Webster's* defines *communication* as "a giving or exchanging of information, signals, or messages as by talk, gestures, or writing."[6] Frankly speaking, God's people need men and women who are going to communicate on a high level of clarity and integrity.

Communication incorporates understanding. It involves a clear exchange and perception of thoughts between speaker and listener. It must also be devoid of vagueness, which distorts the purpose of true communication. To prove what I'm saying, note that most books written for the general public are structured in simple sentences. One does not need an advanced college degree to read the material. Also, great orators have the ability to connect with people by using familiar language. One leaves that event edified and feeling as if one has connected emotionally and cognitively with the speaker.

Speaking in parables, riddles, and enigmas requires an intentional concentration of speaker and listener. If not, people may be left confused. Sometimes the disciples would ask Jesus what He meant after speaking a parable. Our objective is to reach all people, and we (writers and speakers) must communicate clearly what we intend for people to catch.

After many years of preaching and teaching, I have found that it is correctly stated that spiritual things are caught and not taught. Parables and other figurative language may or may not assist in this. When they can't, this creates a major problem because God does speak often in sign language: dreams, visions, and revelations. The Bible says, "All these things Jesus spoke to the multitude in parables; and without a parable He did not speak to them" (Mt. 13:34). There are many sayings behind what is said. The entire Book of the Revelation of Jesus Christ is signified, or in sign language. Most of the signs point to a person: Jesus. This book is not about major cataclysmic events outside of Him. If we take the license to literalize every word, we'll rob ourselves of precious truths. Jesus said, "The words that I speak unto you, they are spirit, and they are life" (Jn. 6:63b KJV).

Sadly, many modern Christians are lacking in the fundamentals of biblical interpretation necessary to understand the Bible. Everything explained in the New Testament is contained in the Old Testament. Consequently, some believers are poorly prepared to function as Kingdom citizens for the twenty-first century cause. Many are need-driven, mundane, lethargic, and mostly settled in mediocrity. Our motivation is not a burning passion for God and a clear pursuit of His Word. Rather, like Israel, we still understand God vicariously through others' experiences.

Some righteous man or woman must stand in the counsel of the Almighty and hear from God for us. It passes down as commentaries, books, and research materials from past epochs or dispensations. Basically, there is nothing wrong with informing ourselves about previous moves of God; however, it does not keep us current. These tools allow us to know where God has been. We must ask ourselves, "Where are we in the present economy of God? Where are the scholars and students of the Spirit that can clearly decode and articulate the present emphasis of God?"

I believe they are beginning to emerge out of the rubble and ashes of the dealings of God. Until God blesses a man by breaking him, he has nothing profitable to disclose. What was once considered burnt stones and broken vessels by religion will become some of the most prolific writers and spokesmen of the current move of God. Much to His delight God chooses those who are considered ignorant and unlearned to confound those who think they are wise.

According to Isaiah, the prophet, God always brings beauty out of ashes. Their resumés may not consist of theological degrees; however, these radical, radiant stalwarts of faith will be consistently marked with this truth: *They have been with Jesus.* Therefore, they have been qualified to speak with and to God's people. And like Peter and John in the early Church, they will speak with clear understanding and conviction.

TIMING AND SEASONS

The second lesson was equally valuable. I have come to understand that the best writers and clarions are always those men and women able to discern the timing of God. The Bible is clear that nothing happens in God until the fullness of time. Even the birth of the Savior was not until time was full. Time runs concurrent with the purpose of the Lord. When God speaks, we may ask, why now, and how will it be accomplished? Our Father does not speak out of season, and He does not waste words. His voice is always consistent with His nature, purpose, and times.

Consider the man Moses. He accomplished nothing until he was within the appointed season of God. He made valiant attempts to assist God *out of season* but to no avail. The New Testament calls the right season a *kairos* moment. Outside of the *kairos* moment Moses attempted to fuse the power of God without the revelation of God. He had to understand that taking needed action is not as important as taking needed action within the *correct season* of God. When a man or woman is resolved to behave in this manner, God will use those whom we think are victimized by an unfair system of slavery to portray our poor decisions. Moses also came to realize failure is never permanent unless one chooses never to take action again. Failure is God's transportation to drive us into the wilderness to have a deeper brokenness worked into our lives.

Exodus, chapters 3–4, set forth the *kairos* moment in Moses' life. A *kairos* moment brings Heaven and Earth together. It is used some 54 times in the singular form, almost always indicating either a set or proper time, season, or occasion.[7] It is also used two times as "opportunity," bespeaking the possibility of something in God never achieved before but now achievable. Earth becomes fully inundated with the wishes of Heaven during a *kairos* moment. It becomes impossible to resist the desires of our sovereign God. His grace produces a new thing in the Earth: God's power and revelation are framed into the same sequence of events.

A cursory look at Moses within the set time of God is compulsory. This period of his life commences with vision. God's idea of vision is that someone must become the embodiment of the vision to complement it. His goal is to reach out and apprehend battered, broken people with a cause greater than themselves or their rotten condition. The

27

writer of Proverbs declares perishing people need relatable, directive vision.

There must come forth a prophetic decree that snaps the chains of the unrelenting shackles of death. Men and women of vision, of course, identify with people of pain and have a great advantage in this. These qualified vessels provide a ray of light in the midst of gross darkness. All of this is conceivable once touched by the hands of the Master. The person God has selected as a visionary conjoins Heaven and Earth by properly responding. It is just a powerful vision until the chosen vessel pauses and receives the reality of the heavenly vision. Visionaries are sustained over the course of time by the vision.

A sovereign God will speak once we have chosen to participate in His purposes by altering our previous course of action. Moses turned aside to behold the vision. The vision became a voice, but not limited to time. Once again, the writer of Hebrews said Moses saw the Eternal One. (See Hebrews 12:18-21.) Therefore, the vision had an eternal quality. We must now turn aside as well. God has many important things to say. Some of them are for temporal conditions and others are for eternity. Preoccupation with what He once said or did cannot be a priority. Who among us will provide Him an ear for now?

Moses was sent as an ambassador of good news. Spiritual protocol required him to know two extremely important truths: 1) who he was, and 2) who sent him! Both the first and last Adam were confronted with whether they knew the same. Most of our success in God lies in how we process these points. If one cannot answer these critical questions, one is definitely not prepared for Kingdom action. It is impossible to represent someone you do not know experientially. When there is no history, there can be no trust. True Kingdom authority has for its backdrop a fundamental foundation of *who sent you*, and *whose you are.*

Broken after 40 years on the backside of the wilderness, Moses was about to become an esteemed statesman of

God. He would go to Egypt with a message directly from God to reform a deformed nation. Four hundred years of Egyptian servitude had ravished Israel's psyche to the point of immobilization. They had lost their dignity, direction, and sense of purpose. Estranged from God, one could easily identify the dehumanization slavery had thrust upon them.

The timing was ripe—sufficiently advanced for reformation of the Old Testament nation. Reformation brings a nation directly into an awareness of the link they are between the forefathers and the succeeding generations. It also alters the impoverished condition of a nation brought on by the imbalances of slavery. The state of that enslaved people's economy changes during reformation for the advancement of Kingdom purposes. Whereas the nation was once poverty-stricken and inadequate for the purposes of God, now it is enriched and empowered to do exploits. Reformation establishes a new sense of authority and spiritual equipment in order to fulfill one's destiny.

In maintaining Kingdom order, Moses was equally a model of a man of God submitting to higher earthly authorities, obtaining a blessing, and then moving swiftly into his destiny during the time of reformation. He did seek release from Jethro, his father-in-law, out of courtesy and respect for his paternal position. However, he had to correct personal disobedience before God fully released him. (See Exodus 4:18-25.) When we have an understanding of covenant and our children are still under our guidance and care, God refuses to consummate His own purposes in our lives when we willfully disobey and refuse to mark our own children with covenantal identity. In those days, one could not represent a covenantal God and break covenant at the same time. Just as then, willful acts of disobedience may delay the fulfillment of a prophetic word in our lives today.

Moses' experiences assure God's timing and purpose will not fail. He will speak clearly and precisely at the right moment. In fact, experience has taught me it is far better for

Him to speak without our interference. Our prayer life may consist of volumes of words, and often God will just wait for us to cease from our labors before anything noteworthy can be discussed. Modern man's lack of understanding has neutralized the efficiency of his prayer life and made it plethoric.

Once in His presence, what can we say that we have not said before? It is high time to simply stop talking and listen. Tendering the words of Habakkuk, "But the Lord is in His holy temple, let all the earth keep silence before Him" (Hab. 2:20). It is rare that Christians desist from human busyness long enough to quiet themselves in the presence of the Lord. And when we do, it is certainly better to listen to Him. If He does not speak, essentially, we have nothing to say other than parroting what has been spoken to someone else. Truthfully, we have nothing to communicate except that first and foremost God communicates with us. If we compound our observations, communication within God's timing is probably the most important lesson to learn.

I have said it, and I will say it again: Most responsible Christians realize that business-as-usual, status-quo Christianity is a foregone conclusion. *It cannot work!* We are now and have been in massive, mind-boggling transition for some time. The purpose of transition is to thrust the Church out of every spiritual, mental, and structural operation inconsistent with the present emphasis of the Holy Spirit. When the Church retains old structures, transition is inevitable. The action of transition allows us to realign with God and to remove that which has become outdated.

Transition will last until we fully detach ourselves from the old thing and attach to the new. God is tearing down and overhauling the Church just as an auto mechanic would thoroughly overhaul an engine. Every part of the engine is adjusted. I use the word *thorough* here because it truly reflects what is happening. Everything about the Church as a community of believers is being adjusted. Paul labored in pain for the Galatians' Church again and again until Christ was formed in her. (See Galatians 4:19.)

Formed is translated from the Greek word *morphoo*, which means "to form, fashion, originally used of artists who shape their material into an image."[8] It expresses the necessity of a change in character and conduct to correspond with an inward spiritual condition in order that there may be moral conformity to Christ. In 1980, at Praise Tabernacle's School of Ministry, I preached that the Church needs *an adjusted vision*. Little did I know that this would be a lingering prophetic word. We are not only in times of renewal, revival, refreshing, and restoration, but something far greater. The Church is equally in a time of reformation. Reformation is a divine overhaul: The Church is examined and judged thoroughly for needed repairs.

Each of the aforementioned moves of God is a precursor to reformation. Sometimes we enjoy the moves of God so much, we fail to comprehend their purposes. We are enthralled by various manifestations of God's presence, such as laughter, and fail to hear what God is speaking to us in the sign. In essence revival ultimately points to a need for reformation. Revival will touch us individually or corporately as the Church, whereas reformation touches the nation and the nations. Which would you rather have? You see, we can be in revival and the nation can still be sinking spiritually, morally, and ethically. A brief study of the history of revival will prove this fact.

Revival brings the dead Church back to life. Its purpose is always temporary. With no malice intended, that unquestionably is its purpose. The true spirit of revival is to bring to life again what was once alive. It comes from the Latin word *revivere* and means "to live again." *Re* is a prefix indicating again.[9] This is an action that was once taken. Subsequently, revival is a statement from God that the Church needs to repeat her first works. He returns us to *His life*! In new birth and the baptism of the Holy Spirit, we should already possess that. Many times our problem is that we fail to act upon Paul's admonition to be continually filled with the Holy Spirit.

On the other hand, reformation shakes us to the core of our being nationally and internationally, producing a new kind of wineskin that is conducive to the present emphasis of the Holy Spirit. Because our focus is, "Go ye into all the world" (Mk. 16:15 KJV), we must be concerned with what moves the nations. That is why the Holy Spirit has impregnated me with the ethos of reformation. Many other servants of God are trumpeting this same sound, especially in developing nations.

Respectfully, other men and women of God may be as strongly persuaded to preach revival as the ultimate solution. That's fine. Our warfare is not against each other. I bless each of them as they move in obedience to the Lord. Intrinsically, revivals are the first signposts of imminent reformation. They are like a hand and glove fitting perfectly together. Brethren are not necessarily on different frequencies, only different portions of the same frequency. Reformation is highly unlikely without some type of individual renewal. Whatever our tasks, we are commanded to do them as unto the Lord. Notwithstanding, I am fully persuaded about the need for reformation.

THE READER

The third consideration is the audience reading this book. I trust the vast majority of my readers will be hungry, concerned people, interested in the advancement of mankind. To you, I say we direly need reformation in our world. A war is going on in our cities, townships, nations, and continents. Wicked spiritual assailants have set themselves against everything we cherish and hold dear: our values, our morals, our liberties, and especially our seed. The embankment has been set. All can hear the thundering hooves of wicked steeds in every sector of society. The ominous enemy, the flesh man with erroneous ideas, is defeated, yet locked in battle with uninformed Christians. Two opposing kingdoms with very different agendas are vying for the same turf: control of the nations! The commander-in-chief,

King Jesus, has already provided the winning strategy. It is the reality of His *finished work*. We must, as instruments of God, release the victory of Heaven into the Earth.

It will take the reformed Church, all of us, to accomplish on a practical level what Jesus won for us two thousand years ago. Our separate, isolated visions will not stop the flood of increasing iniquity in our nations if we, as Christ's Church, remain disconnected. A vast majority of our communities are inundated with diabolical hordes. The antichrist spirit has been stirred up into a nervous frenzy. Terrorism is everywhere—in the Church and the world! No so-called sanctuary is completely safe, not even those with sophisticated alarm systems. The spirit of division has left the Church in all nations naked and exposed. None other than Jesus said, "Every kingdom divided against itself is brought to desolation, and every city or house divided against itself will not stand" (Mt. 12:25b). Was He right in His observation? Of course He was. Our polished, educated intellect cannot deliver us this time.

Two major waves of reformation have occurred. One began with Martin Luther in the early sixteenth century, and the other with the neo-Pentecostals in the early twentieth century. The final phase of reformation is to bring us into the truth of "In whom ye also are builded together for an habitation of God through the Spirit" (Eph. 2:22 KJV). The emphasis will be fullness in the body for the fullness of times.

Previous reformations have brought us thus far. The pioneers of reformation realized God had begun a work in and through them, but it had to be finished. John Calvin, the renowned Swiss reformer, made it clear: The sixteenth-century Church must continue to reform, although it had a fantastic yet challenging and sometimes chilling start. The upper crust of Romanism had become weak, corrupt, and dysfunctional; and the forerunners of the Reformation had chipped away at the brittle condition of Roman Catholicism.

Initially the Reformation was a statement against hierarchical, absolute rulers and tyranny.

Martin Luther sheared the upper echelon of Roman Catholicism and addressed its lifeless clericalism. Afterwards he set up a new wineskin (the Lutheran Church), functional and secure, built upon the truth "the just shall live by faith" (Rom. 1:17b). After the death of Martin Luther in 1546 most reformers who were thoroughly persuaded of papacy errors looked to Calvin for prophetic direction and keen leadership. Standing in his measure, Calvin taught the whole counsel of God, as he understood it almost five hundred years ago. He was like a masterful architect. His acute mind enabled him to read details into the plan and establish specifications that still influence fundamental theology today.

The final phase of reformation will also happen in a Church dedicated to change. She must be free of meaningless prejudices of every kind. Christians will be uniquely joined and anointed to bring healing and empowerment to the nations. Some of our most meaningful experiences will be with people who are of different colors and cultures. Out of our compounding will come great exploits for the Kingdom. The psalmist declares that unity of the brethren is like "precious ointment upon the head." (See Psalm 133:1-2 KJV.) The reformed Church will be "holy anointing oil" that destroys the bondage of satanic strategies and strongholds over our nations.

I have often wondered what the landscape of our nations would be like if we truly became one in purpose. I am speaking of a collegiality of brethren who understand the value and advantage of flowing together, especially beyond the walled cities of race, culture, and denominational ties. Just in case this thought signals caution in your mind, I am not speaking of dissolving distinctions that create diversity and uniqueness within the Christian community. However, we can accomplish our assignment much better than any *one* of us can. Collectively we have the task of presenting Christ in His fullness to our generation.

Undoubtedly this is best accomplished within the framework of diversity. So, it is not uniformity that I am advocating, although uniformity provides a basic comfort to brethren who thrive on sameness. Diversity is really what God uses to stretch us in relationships. From time to time He challenges us to pull up the stakes of our present existence and stretch the limits of our horizons. The spirit of reformation aids us in doing this. We are hurled into a new level of faith.

A few years ago our Father chastised me because I was selfish and lacked a *WE consciousness*. He challenged me with two questions. First, did I believe every single pastor was equally called to function in the Kingdom of God just as I was? If yes, then why don't I pray for their ministries just as much as my own? Suddenly, to my own amazement and embarrassment, I had to confront my own arrogant idealism and religious snobbishness.

When I now say, "We are the people of God," it takes on a completely different meaning. The significance of this statement is that it means all of God's people everywhere! Unfortunately pride will cause us to disrespect some of the Lord's children—it is such a fragile, haughty mountain. When we think too highly of ourselves, we may be blocked from experiencing some of our greatest encounters in God. It is humbling to realize that no one Church group or nation, particularly the one I serve and live in, can give the community and nations everything they need.

However, each Church has a unique thumbprint and a special assignment from the Lord to the community and the nation. Every nation has a predetermined boundary of reflection in God, thus complementing other nations in revealing the true image of God. Together we can do greater things as co-laborers with the Lord.

Time has taught me that a writer must have a prepared hearer for what is being said. Without hesitation, I would say that if you have this book, you are a prepared hearer. It beats hurling stones and flinging arrows of accusation against one another. By allowing me to flow into your thought processes concerning this matter of reformation, we can release an anointing that totally thwarts every desire and strategy of the carnal, soulish, and devilish domain. The sleeping giant, the Church, must awaken. God will empower us as we pass through the valley of humility and brokenness. (See Proverbs 15:33.)

Reformation is best served through a corporate vision, a corporate anointing, and a mature leadership who has the current pulse of God's heart. Leadership is influence. Leaders fan the flames of reformation in the hearts of others. Because of their penchant for unity, division is absolutely unacceptable. I propose that it is time to cast down the accuser of the brethren rather than the brethren. May we become, in practice, one Church? God sees us as one body fused together by the presence of Christ in our midst.

In summary, before any army goes to war the high military brass will formulate a strategy for victory. The purpose behind the plan is to identify the swiftest way to victory with the least amount of casualties and without forfeiting the predetermined goals. The Godhead established a victorious strategy before the foundation of the world. (See Ephesians 1:4-10.) Now the reality of the Heavens must be downloaded into the Earth. Godly men and women must come into agreement with Heaven's purpose.

I would encourage you to read this book carefully. If you have somehow received it, that tells me that you are either curious, or maybe fully persuaded about the need for reformation, as many others have concluded. Whatever the case may be, you have the book now. I implore you to make good use of it. Allow the Holy Spirit to speak to your heart. Possibly, this book may place you on a deeper journey into Him. As Paul declared, you are yet to apprehend what you have been apprehended for. (See Philippians 3:12.) In Him, there will always be a fresh awareness of your purpose. If this book moves you to that place, all praises to God.

ENDNOTES

1. Adapted from Sinclair B. Ferguson, J. I. Packer, and David F. Wright, *New Dictionary of Theology* (England; Downers Grove, IL): InterVarsity Press, 1988), 276.

2. Adapted from Infoplease.com, *Roundup of Recent Discoveries*, 2001 (The Learning Network Inc., 2001), 3.

3. *Webster's New World College Dictionary*, Third Edition, Victoria Neufeldt, ed. (New York: Simon & Schuster, Inc., 1997), 1421.

4. James Strong, "Greek Dictionary of the New Testament," *The New Strong's Exhaustive Concordance of the Bible* (Nashville: Thomas Nelson Publishers, 1984), # 4832.

5. Stephen Everett, *The Mystery of Melchisedec* (Shippensburg, PA: Destiny Image, 1991).

6. *Webster's*, 282.

7. James Strong, "Greek Dictionary of the New Testament," *The New Strong's Complete Dictionary of Bible Words* (Nashville: Thomas Nelson Publishers, 1996), #2540.

8. Spiros Zodhiates, Th.D., ed., "Lexical Aids to the New Testament," *The Hebrew-Greek Key Word Study Bible* (Chattanooga, TN: AMG Publishers, 1991), #3445.

9. Webster's, 1149.

Chapter One

THE SOUND THAT CHANGED EVERYTHING

When the Day of Pentecost had fully come, they were all with one accord in one place.

And suddenly there came a sound from heaven, as of a rushing mighty wind, and it filled the whole house where they were sitting.

And when this sound occurred, the multitude came together, and were confused, because everyone heard them speak his own language.

Acts 2:1-2,6

In the early 1970s our church in Jacksonville, North Carolina, relocated from one neighborhood to another. Without acquiring the services of professional architects or contractors, we built our new facilities debt-free. (There were skilled carpenters and masons among us, with plenty of laborers willing to assist.) Our leader, the late apostle Lewis Sanders, was a very astute businessman and skillful in the areas of monetary stewardship. Through his adept guidance, we were on our way!

Shortly after coming into our new church home in 1972, God began to adjust our theology. We began to hear a *new sound*. I remember Pastor Sanders saying, "What we had was good, but there is more in God for us, and somehow we must find it!" It all began with a jovial, apostolic brother named Paul Gaskins, from Washington D.C. He taught us the necessity of being established in present truth. As Pentecostals, our arrogance led us to believe we had all the truth, which is totally uncharacteristic of the in-part

Pentecostal theology! In-part simply means Pentecost is the earnest or downpayment of our spiritual heritage. (See Ephesians 1:14; Second Corinthians 5:5.) A downpayment is a guarantee of a much greater expression in the future. God cocooned us for a short time and taught us the principles of the new day. I remember the difficulty of being in obscurity, sheltered away from groups we used to fellowship with. Our church had become the odd ball, as it were, and subject to much ridicule.

We were introduced to many Bible study manuals from Bible Temple, now known as City Bible Church in Portland, Oregon. Also, we studied Graham Truscott's *The Power of His Presence*, which is a wonderful treatise on the restoration of the Tabernacle of David. Because we were making a transition from a Pentecostal style of worship to what was cutting-edge in God, even our worship services changed dramatically. Many of us read books like Merlin Carothers' *Prison to Praise* and *Power in Praise.* We were in a constant state of repentance and not totally sure why. Paul Gaskins taught on *repentance from dead works* for weeks. We had to reluctantly face the narrow "isms" and mean-spirited (at times) approach to our Pentecostal faith. The more he taught, the more we repented and experienced brokenness.

God used this trumpet sound to get us on our way. Little did we know this was to be a sound that would change everything. Our approach to worship and praise was divinely interrupted, and our theology was blown to pieces. We had to rethink the wineskin. In those days we really didn't understand that God doesn't pour new wine into old wineskins. In this link of transition, our assembly was being prepared for something much greater that would come three years later. Each change we made inaugurated a new wave of glory in the things of God. God was about to introduce us to men who would make a certain sound that required ears to hear them. Again, little did we know that it would be *a sound that changed everything*!

WHY SOUND?

Absolutely nothing changes in the Earth until our heavenly Father releases the sound of permission. Sound is most crucial to everything God does. It is the vibration of His voice distinctly heard, received, and understood by someone. In fact, *Webster's II Dictionary* gives one of the definitions of *sound* as "a vibratory disturbance in the pressure and density of a fluid or in the elastic strain in a solid."[1] For the sake of simplicity, sound is a vibration that disturbs. God disturbs our normal routine each time He makes a new sound. Just as a sound can also be a relatively large body of water connecting two larger bodies of water, God's sound is the prophetic interlude between different seasons. This book will combine both of these thoughts together.

In order for the Kingdom of God to advance, God must disturb what we think we know and are hearing and especially what we're doing. None other than Jesus said, "My sheep hear my voice, and I know them, and they follow me" (Jn. 10:27). Everything in God commences with vision accompanied by the sound of His voice. His voice sounds concurrently with His manifestation of Himself. God is light, and light is indicative of His presence! When light moves into our sphere, the noise of its speed becomes sound. Revelation 4:5a says, "And out of the throne proceeded lightnings and thunderings and voices." There were a multitude of voices on Mount Sinai, a multitude of voices in the upper room on the Day of Pentecost, and there will be a multitude of voices in the Feast of Tabernacles. (See Revelation 19:6-8.) God always announces the new thing He's doing in the languages of the existing nations all at once, thus making a multitudinous sound.

Note the order: lightning before thundering. Even in our atmosphere, lightning precedes thunder. However, thunder completes the sound package. Interlocked in this thought is the fact that every time God moves, God talks. Note these examples:

- The sound of the Lord God walking in the Garden. (See Genesis 3:8.)
- The sound of the Lord's voice on Mount Sinai. (See Exodus 19:16-19.)
- The sound of the Jubilee trumpet. (See Leviticus 25:9.)
- The sound of the trumpet before the assault on Jericho. (See Joshua 6:5,20.)
- The sound that rent the Earth at Solomon's coronation. (See First Kings 1:37-41.)
- There is a sound of an abundance of rain. (See First Kings 18:41.)
- The sound of the mighty rushing wind on the Day of Pentecost. (See Acts 2:2,6.)

Each of these examples facilitated a new day in the economy of God for the people of God. In each case, without exception, suddenly everything changed. These were sounds that changed everything. Many more examples could have been chosen to exclaim this same truth; however, this short list should serve the purpose.

HEAVEN'S DOWNLOAD

When the Heavens break forth as the voice of God, in computer language, a significant download comes to Earth. Because of self-deception with our own importance to the Kingdom of God, it is not unusual to think God is responding to our efforts. Somehow we think we have twisted His arm and made Him meet our selfish expectations. However, this is never true and comes close to tempting the Almighty. Temptation is trying to get God to do something inconsistent with His will. Fortunately, we can never manipulate or control God like that.

A more careful study of Scripture reveals that God moves and speaks to covenantal people in agreement with His own unchangeable time clocks. There are three of them summed up in the Feasts of the Lord: the Feast of Passover, the Feast of Pentecost, and the Feast of Tabernacles. (See Exodus 23:14-17 and Deuteronomy 16:16.) There is a literal and spiritual fulfillment of each: the literal in the Old Covenant nation Israel, and the spiritual in the New Covenant nation, the Church.

Acts 2 happens to be one of those timely downloads from God. The time was ripe, and the Day of Pentecost had fully come, not partially come. The outward indicator that things in God's economy are matured is the suddenness by which everything happens. Strong's *Greek Dictionary of the New Testament* reveals that *suddenly* means "unawares, unexpectedly, non-apparent, and that which is not manifest."[2] Simply speaking, what God was about to do had never happened before. No human face had been formed to the new idea in God's heart yet. Moving strictly from the ideal of biblical manifestation, God's hand was yet to swarm over mankind in impartation. The Feast of Passover already had its God/man face: Jesus. The Bible says, "For indeed Christ, our Passover, was sacrificed for us" (1 Cor. 5:7b). Now Pentecost, a different offering, must find its man-face, which proves to be corporate.

NEW HEAVENLY MANIFESTATION

The 120 people in the upper room on the Day of Pentecost are caught squarely in the midst of a new heavenly manifestation. It would not be over-exaggeration to call this a kind of heavenly nuclear blast. Did they know what to expect? Probably no more than the current Church knows. Ready or not, we are about to be blasted out of our complacency. In fact, the most spiritual one of those in the upper room was probably completely blown away by what God did. However, they became the corporate man of God in the Earth. Henceforth, God's man will continue to be many-membered and gender inclusive. Men and women, all with previous alliances and persuasions, were in that upper room.

First Corinthians 15:5-7 says, "and that He was seen by Cephas, and then by the twelve, After that he was seen by over five hundred brethren at once, of whom the greater part remain to the present, but some have fallen asleep. After that He was seen by James; and then by all the apostles." Why not all five hundred in the upper room? Certainly a great crowd would have meant a greater endorsement from God. We seem to associate nickels and noses with the favor of God. At least that is how we think in the modern Church, being more fully persuaded by quantity than quality. A quick trip in the Book of Genesis reveals the number 120 as meaning the end of all flesh. (See Genesis 6:3.) In applying the law of first use, God was announcing the end of one order and the beginning of another on the Day of Pentecost. God does not end anything without the seed of the new being extracted out of the old. He was permanently ending a dispensation that had lasted for 15 hundred years.

Obediently, this apprehensive contingency had kept the command of Jesus to wait until they were endued with power from on high. And endued they were! Although this was a corporate experience, yet it was individualized in each of them. They were filled with the Holy Spirit and each person spoke in tongues. Paul called this experience "the blessing of Abraham" (Gal. 3:14).

When Abraham's name changed from Abram to Abraham, it was the Hebrew breath sound added to his name. Consequently, it was also the breath or Spirit of God that gendered change on the Day of Pentecost. As with our father Abraham, so it is with the New Testament believer. The Spirit of God changes our name or nature, and what a powerful exchange this is!

What an extraordinary sound! The consummation of the waiting period had ended and the inauguration of the new age had begun. It gathered the multitude, and at the same time confused and perplexed them. It completely cut against the grain of what was anticipated during the festive season. They were in Jerusalem to celebrate and recycle the previous economy of God and His commands.

Mankind seems to excel in the art of recycling—passing through a cycle, creating a rut, and doing the same thing over and over again. Yes, we are famous for constructing institutions out of one-time encounters. In the meantime God is doing a new thing. If we will just listen, He will inform us and allow us to participate.

ETERNITY'S ECHO

In Acts 2:2 the word *sound* is the Greek word *echos*.[3] Immediately one can see the English word *echo*. An echo is the repetition of sound by reflection of sound waves from a surface. God's immutable surface is His incorruptible will and desire. According to Bible dictionaries, God's will is His deliberate design. God's design is what He has conceived in His mind. So, there is a definite intentional factor in everything God does.

God's voice from the Heavens resounds what had already been predetermined in eternity in the Inter-Theistic Covenant. (Inter-Theistic is the agreement the Father, Son, and Holy Spirit had about everything before there was anything.) The Law, the schoolmaster, had also indicated this same sound in Israel's birth as a covenantal nation and her annual convocations. The Inter-Theistic Covenant, which includes the Old and New Covenants, defines the scope of what God had envisioned in His vast heart. The Father, Son, and Holy Spirit were in perfect harmony. They were actually the first "Amen." Rumored in the Heavens for ages, God's desire was finally manifesting in Earth. The earthly theatre of the upper room becomes the audio-visual of the manifest presence of God just as Mount Sinai had many centuries earlier. (See Exodus 19:18-19; Deuteronomy 5:22.)

This seemingly unimportant crew had become the first-fruits of God's new order. Peter's preaching indicated many others would follow. If any one of them were asked to clearly define their expectation in detail before the experience, they could not. Often God will give an experience, and then He will explain what He has done. Evidence in age after age proves God has gratified Himself in moving this way.

From the human standpoint, faith is needed to embrace something one cannot logically explain. Particularly for the twenty-first century Western man, this may be a bit much. Remember, we think we have all the solutions until one of them does not work. We are known for measuring things with our heads and not our hearts. However, if we are hungry for God, faith is the highway that leads to Him. The writer of Hebrews still echoes these age-abiding words, even after 20 centuries, "But without faith it is impossible to please Him, for he who comes to God must believe that He is, and that He is a rewarder of those who diligently seek Him" (Heb. 11:6).

The Church in the upper room was seeking God. Seeking is time-consuming, but they had an expectation of God fulfilling His Word. As they sought God, He rewarded them. God paid their wages, for reward means to pay wages. Because the Church has come to the end of many renewals and revivals, it is time to become passionate about seeking God for reformation. Most of what we have called modern revival produced very limited results. In the imagery of the prophet Ezekiel, revivals and renewals produce waters at the ankle and knee levels. Waters to swim in await diligent seekers. (See Ezekiel 47:1-5.)

The next wave of God will be humanly uncontrollable. God has promised to move, and man will not be able to place Him into some denominational or non-denominational device. Visualize, if you will, a release from God that man's strength cannot steady, a move of God so pure that nothing can defile it! Now, you may be saying, "That's wishful thinking—when man has polluted everything God has allowed him to participate in thus far!" Such will not be the case this time, because too much is at stake. God has a wave of glory that will dismiss our history and propensity for failure.

HISTORICAL PENTECOST

Historically, Pentecost was about the firstfruits of the wheat harvest being presented to the Lord in the Temple. The offering consisted of two loaves—representing Jew and Gentile—baked with leavened flour. (See Leviticus 23:17.) The Levitical High Priest would pour oil on the loaves and bake them early in the morning. Christ, the High Priest over the house of God, poured oil on the Jewish loaf in Acts 2 and on the representative Gentile loaf in Acts 10. Leaven speaks of the fact that the baptism of the Holy Spirit was not because people were perfect; it was a baptism that would lead into perfection. In this firstfruits presentation, God's providence was celebrated at the beginning of the wheat season.

It is important to know that every major festival in Israel's history was associated with a major historical event in forming them as a people group. God commanded them to gather three times in a year. (See Deuteronomy 16:16.) Passover, celebrating the Exodus from Egypt, has a wonderful theme: the creation of the nation as a sovereign entity. At best, they were displaced nomads in Egypt. Pentecost, which was fifty days after the Passover, has the theme of *revelation*. On the basis of Exodus 19:1, historians deduce that God actually gave the Law on the Day of Pentecost. The Feast of Tabernacles, commemorating 40 years of wandering in the wilderness, culminated by entering the Promised Land. It has the theme of *full redemption*.[4]

For the last two thousand years, the Church has been a Pentecostal economy. It is high time to go on to maturity. What was thought to be full Gospel in the mid-twentieth century was in fact two-thirds Gospel at best. In the strictest sense of the word *Pentecost*, it is 50 percent Gospel. Pentecost is 50 days after Passover and advances us about halfway in our destiny. Paul calls it the earnest payment. (See Second Corinthians 1:22; 5:5; Ephesians 1:14.)

The Expanded Vine's Expository Dictionary tells us that *earnest* is translated from the Greek word *arrabon*. Originally, it was a Phoenician word introduced into Greece meaning "earnest-money deposited by the purchaser and forfeited if the purchase was not completed." In modern Greek *arrabona* is an engagement ring.[5] God pledged Himself in Pentecost to practically outwork man's total redemption. Christ's finished work was the divine guarantee of this. In the words of my dear friend, Kelley Varner, "Passover frees us; Pentecost fills us; and Tabernacles fulfills us." Total freedom occurs in the redemption of our bodies.

A New Thing

We, the Church, must break out of our dilapidated cisterns that contain no water and return to the Fountain of Living Waters. Why? Because God is doing a new thing. We have partisan differences, diversity somewhat, fleshly soul ties everywhere, but very little unity. In Acts 2, there definitely was unity with diversity. They were of one mind and interests—period. Many Christians have come to appreciate and value diversity because it does not diminish unity; in fact, it enhances it. The Scripture says, "They were all with one accord" (Acts 2:1). "One accord" is the compound word *homothumadon*, an adverb from a composition meaning "unanimously." Each word part is so replete with meaning. *Homos* means "at the same place or time," and *thumos* means "passion (as if breathing hard) resulting from the fires of sacrifice."[6] Jehovah's determinate counsel sacrificed Jesus, and He became the fulfillment of the Old Testament burnt offering. Because of that truth, they were in the same place with the same passion—a passion for Him!

In their diversified unity, Acts 1 and 2 corroborate several ideals about the first disciples:

1. Men and women are ministry-conscious and never title-conscious. (See Acts 1:21-26.) That alone eliminated

the spirit of competition that would have easily fueled disastrous consequences in the new thing God was doing. Today, the appetites men have for titles is amazing. Inherent in this are many unresolved insecurity issues and woeful competitive traps waiting to ensnare the seeker. What's important is to discover what God has written about you in the Lamb's Book of Life. Titles lead to status, and status is static and nonorganic. The Kingdom of God is not about pecking order and social rank—it is about function. Function is ministry; the two are inseparable. Whereas status leads to brokered, political posturing; brokenness leads to ministry. The first disciples were ministry-conscious because they were broken men and women.

2.   This new servant/leadership team was composed of men and women of many different backgrounds and temperaments (See Acts 1:13.) Since leadership is influence, who would you rather influence you? Kingdom servants or Kingdom scholars? Even the inner circle, Peter, James, and John, were very different in personality and temperament; but they were all servants and refused to usurp authority over God's heritage. No one was a clone or imitation of someone else. The New Testament reveals one kind of leadership—servant leadership. (See Matthew 20:20-28.) The apostles gladly called themselves servants of God. Gentiles were and still are lords over people. Conversely, Kingdom authority finds its vestment in serving. Attitudinally, there could never be an abuse of authority when servants minister with a true understanding of their roles.

3.   The male/female question is not problematic. Both genders are welcomed in the upper room. (See Acts 1:14.) In the purity and unity of the moment, gender prejudice was excommunicated. One way to gauge a true move of God is: Are women included as equal partners with men in the move? Many wonderful books have been written about the equality that the Dispensation of

Grace has given the female. Women can no longer be treated as second-class citizens in the Kingdom. As a man, if you are confusing the careful instructions of Paul in First Timothy 2:8-12 regarding husbands and wives with male superiority in the Kingdom, this is absolutely wrong! God's image can only be rightly revealed in a male/female, equal-partner relationship.

4.   The new thing God is doing does not create the two-caste system of clergy and laity either. In fact, where does this idea come from? There is no clergy and laity in the upper room, as we understand the modern concept of clergy and laity. Everyone needed the baptism of the Holy Spirit to do the works of Jesus. (It will be clear that functionally God uses the ministry gifts of Ephesians 4:11 as instruments of empowerment without compromising the functionality of the whole Body of Christ. Ministry gifts must always work to replace themselves to prevent heavy authoritarian structures.) The very thought of clergy and laity is an aberration of the all-believer priesthood espoused by the apostles. (See First Peter 2:9.) Less than two centuries after Pentecost, the concept of the priesthood of all believers was not understood or acknowledged. Body ministry ceased. The ministers or clergy were the only ones designated as priests. The deceptive root system for the ancient papacy culture and the modern professional pastor was now in place.

God does not endorse such a system because it hinders growth and development in the body. Like a physical body, a spiritual body grows from proper exercise and nutrition. For instance, if I exercise my arms and nothing else, the muscular development in my arms will be well defined. However, the rest of my body will suffer from atrophy. This is precisely what happens in a clergy/laity relationship. The clergy ministers the life of Christ, and therefore develops under the mentorship of the Holy Spirit. The laity, on the other hand, emaciates continuously until someone has the courage to stir them to action through declaring their rightful destiny in God.

DIVINE INTRUSION

Pentecost was a season of divine intrusion into the economy of humanity to terminate one thing and initiate another. During the course of the economy of Law, religious spirits had taken ownership of the things of God. Many traditions of the elders usurped godly commands and instructions. The inspired writers of the New Testament labeled the feasts of the Lord as Jewish possessions, when in reality they belonged to the Lord. (See Leviticus 23:1-4; John 2:13; 5:1; 7:2.) Man had effectively turned a God-centered ideal into a man-centered travesty. It is no different in the modern Church. Today, the Church spends more time dreaming about evacuating the planet—which is unscriptural and in fact, another gospel—than about maturing in Christ.

God ended that order with a divine blast of His breath. The simile "as of a rushing mighty wind" (Acts 2:2b) speaks to the prophetic significance of the moment. God inhaled the obedience, unity, fervent prayers, and the spirit of rest that was upon the 120 before He exhaled. The waiting seekers were sitting. Pentecost did not begin with soulish, carnal sweat from a loud prayer meeting, pitched feverishly to the point of overwhelming God. God is only moved by His purpose. Whenever God breathes, get prepared. Things are blown away, and it's not very encouraging at first. It could be compared to the rotation of a violent whirlwind removing every unnecessary, unproductive superstructure off the foundation. (See Proverbs 10:25.)

The whole affair is generally violent. *Mighty*, found in "a rushing mighty wind" (Acts 2:2b), is translated from the Greek word *biaios*, which means "violent:—mighty; through the idea of vital activity; the present state of existence."[7] Violence suggests the mighty power of God at work. Conclusively, it discloses the certainty of God's unwavering determination to do something new rather than just improving and patching the old. The reason for this is that across the board, the Church appears more as a knowledge-skin than a wineskin. Secondly, most Christians are worn out with the patchwork of new programs feeding the flesh in the old wineskin. Every patch renders the wineskin more brittle and exposes the utter futility of attempting to patch it.

The Acts church became a new wineskin, a kind of first-fruits of all the new generation represented. Nothing other than a violent breath of God could dislodge them mentally from the old paradigm. The prepared vessels were in place. Peter had emerged as the leader of the apostolic leadership team. The mild rebuke of Jesus earlier had settled the team's jockeying for position, power, and prestige. Although only 120 strong, they were one body. This body needed to become animated. Thus, there was a need for the breath of God.

I am reminded of the necessity of the breath of God to animate Adam before he became a living being. (See Genesis 2:7.) He was *formed* but he had no vital life. Also, the army of Ezekiel 37, which is the whole house of Israel and Judah, does not become a living organism until the coming violence of the prophetic breath of Jehovah. The different parts of the body had been revived and gathered from dearth; however, they still needed breath. In this same passage, the calling forth of the four winds of the Earth speaks of the universality of God's intent. Prophetically, it summons us to a global mentality.

There were at least 15 different dialects (see Acts 2:8-11) present when Pentecost fully came. Amazingly, most did not have a clue as to what God was doing, just as many do not today. They were stuck, busy recycling what God used to do; and it would be almost sacrilege to consider anything new. It is like men believing today that God can do nothing new because of the canonization of the Scripture. Now, before you stone me, I realize that whatever God does today will be in the spirit of what He has done. He builds and advances from the foundation of the last thing He did. One may ask at this point, "Are you saying God is writing another book with a new generation?" My answer is, "Certainly not!" However, He is adding a twenty-first century line to the Book of Acts through the works of living epistles.

God will not tolerate the aberrant wineskin of the modern Church much longer. She is intoxicated on religious mixture and filled with foolishness and contempt for holiness. We have digested non-biblical traditions, such as disunity of the body and sectarianism, which cause the Body of Christ to be ineffective before the world. Tremors and shakings are everywhere in the Earth, with heavenly sound waves rippling to and fro. Any country one would visit will have all the spiritual, social, political, and economic indicators that God has arisen with vigor. After spending some time recently preaching in North and South America, South Africa, Central America, and Asia, I can tell you without hesitation that God has tailored certain shakings to every nation. It's not just America—it's the whole Earth. The harvest of the Earth is ripe.

We cannot fake His presence with polished promotions and high-tech hype forever. Like the 120 in the upper room, it is high time to come aside. Hear the command of Jesus. Let's move away from the hustle and bustle, high energy, and busyness of clever religiousness. What's at stake? Meeting and embracing a holy God at the point of new beginnings. A holy remnant is being ushered into a new kind of upper room to be caught up into a new dimension of Kingdom activity that will jar the Church out of her complacency. God truly desires a body, a matured son, to be co-laborers together with Him.

JUST WHO WILL PARTICIPATE?

Our concepts of participation must be adjusted. In every age of mankind, God sought for those who would participate in sovereignty. He places the seed of His doings in a remnant to be expanded into a multitude. In this new dimension, all believers become spiritually qualified participants and not just paid professionals. They must do the work of the ministry. For this reason alone, *everyone* on the initial Day of Pentecost received the baptism of the Holy Spirit. In defining the moment, the apostle Peter said this experience was for as many as the Lord shall call (see Acts 2:39). God the Father was in an empowering mode. God's *ministry aids* in Ephesians 4:11 must do the same today. Rather than the ministry gifts seeking to acquire power, we should seek to empower the Body. The Body of Christ needs a fresh impartation that nurtures in each of us an apostolic/prophetic capacity to hear God's voice. Because God is speaking a fresh *rhema*, we can be built into a new wineskin of expression.

Through books such as Tommy Tenney's *The God Chasers* and *The God Catchers*, much of the Church has shifted consciousness. It was amazing to me how two books articulated the deep hunger of God's people. Many are no longer willing to accept the standard liturgy and play traditional Charismatic trivia, especially when we could live in higher dimensions. Notwithstanding, there is a cry, like the Magi of Matthew 2, demanding to see Him. Nothing other than the need to see Him brought the wise men to Jerusalem—not holy land, holy people, holy preachers, or holy anything. People are conspicuously absent from church services because Jesus is absent. Our services do not allow Him a place of lordship! Why are we afraid for Him to control and exercise headship in His Church? What a sham! It is His Church and He has to be granted entry, and not merely entry but also respect and honor as He rules.

In all honesty, although I am a conference and convention speaker, at times I still go through entire services looking for Jesus. Others, which are hyped to the maximum, leave me asking, "Where is He? Where is He who is Lord and Master of the Church?" Despairingly, I would do anything just to smell His scent in our midst. Promises! Promises! And very little product. After all, it is His Church, and

He has a legal right to be the center of attraction in His Body. The touchstone is a type of black stone formerly used to test the purity of gold or silver by the streak left on it when it was rubbed with the metals. The touchstone that men will measure church services by in the twenty-first century is God's presence. Men and women will be trusted who openly exhibit the presence of God. If God's presence is with them, those who are thirsty and hungry for God will connect with these valuable vessels of God. People will see the Lord in the vessel. If He is with them, those who are led by the Spirit will seek Him out.

PROPHESY FULFILLED

The baptism of the Holy Spirit was Bible prophecy fulfilled. Although freely given by God, it is a subjective experience (subject to the receiver). The explanation was objective and orderly by the Word of God. God magnified His Word. (See Psalm 138:2.) Acts 1 and 2 are replete with confirmations that God fulfills His Word and not one single word falls to the ground. If we are going to substantiate something in the Spirit, we cannot do it by subjectivity alone.

Many heresies and problems have evolved in the Body of Christ over the years through using the faulty method of unchallenged subjectivity. In the final analysis, we must locate what God is doing in His Word. Even before Jesus entered public ministry He located Himself in the Word. (See Luke 4.) As Simon Peter moderated and preached, he quoted the Word. Obviously, as a retired fisherman he was probably a marginal student of the Old Testament prophets and historians. Listen to the passages of Scripture the Holy Spirit quickened to him.

Let their dwelling place be desolate; let no one live in their tents.　　　　　　　　　Psalm 69:25

Let his days be few, and let another take his office.　　　　　　　　　Psalm 109:8

55

And it shall come to pass afterward, that I will pour out My Spirit on all flesh; your sons and your daughters shall prophesy, your old men shall dream dreams, your young men shall see visions.

And also on My menservants and on My maidservants I will pour out My Spirit in those days.

Joel 2:28-29

I have set the Lord always before me; because He is my right hand I shall not be moved.

Therefore my heart is glad, and my glory rejoices; my flesh also will rest in hope.

For You will not leave my soul in Sheol, nor will You allow Your Holy One to see corruption.

You will show me the path of life; in Your presence is fullness of joy; at Your right hand are pleasures forevermore. Psalm 16:8-11

The Lord said to my Lord, "Sit at My right hand, till I make Your enemies Your footstool." Psalm 110:1

From matters concerning Judas the traitor to Jesus the Savior, the Scripture speaks expressly. A new experience is given and then God explains His own gift without the stale, stoic existence of men with formal scholarship. He takes ignorant and unlettered fishermen and places them at the head of the new dispensation. They become chief spokesmen. Standing with the others, Peter gave a valedictory address to the *old order*. The thing of beauty in this is: Not a single one has anything to lose—nor will they take God's glory for themselves. Unqualified people are under no illusions! Talk with any of them. One by one you will hear them heralding that without Jesus and the empowering effectiveness of the Holy Spirit, they can do nothing!

Within the upper room God is doing a new thing—something fresh. Outside the upper room, with great pageantry and fanfare, the same old thing is going on. When I was a boy, sometimes we would challenge an opponent to a fight by drawing a line in the dirt and daring them to cross it. Standing at the edge of that line, one must be prepared to back up all that was spoken. Drawing that line would put courage in cowards. The point is: A line is drawn in the Spirit. Those in the upper room are on one side, and those who are absent are on the other side.

On one side are the things we know everything about—our doctrines, our faith, our disciplines, our songs, our strategies, and all. On the other side are all the things we know very little about other than prophecy. We face this startling question: "Will we choose the old or the new, the fresh or the stale, freedom or bondage, the religious thing or the new relational thing?" Once again, hear the timeless words of Isaiah. They are apropos to our situation today.

> *Do not remember the former things, nor consider the things of old.*
> *Behold, I will do a new thing, now it shall spring forth; shall you not know it? I will even make a road in the wilderness and rivers in the desert.*
>
> Isaiah 43:18-19

It is important to understand that within the context of a *new thing* are *new things.* God remains the same, but He can do new things—new to us! For example, Christ is our Passover. Two thousand years ago that was a new thing. Because of the Passover we enjoy introduction into the New Covenant through new birth, death to the old man, water baptism in the name of the Lord, divine healing, and many other privileges. These are all *new things* because of a new thing.

The same is true concerning the Feast Day of Pentecost. New things are locked within the structure of the new thing. God's process releases a variety of things out of *the thing.* Concerning our future experience of the Feast of Tabernacles, there will also be many new things within the new thing. Every new thing in God exceeds the glory of the former things. That's why God said in Isaiah 43:18, "Do not remember!" (Re)member is to place fragmented members back together again. We must not put the members of old things back together again.

The most difficult command any generation faces is to forget the previous move of God, especially when its blessings are still effectual. Even today men are still attempting to rebuild twentieth-century Pentecostalism. Our brains are filled with Pentecostal track marks from the last thing God accomplished. Science has proven our habits result from track marks on the brain. Let's imagine we could flush the brain of former tracks. It would be easy to reprogram it with new things. Neither old things nor the spirit of old things would come to mind. When something doesn't exist, it is impossible to reflect on or remember it. Remembering validates the rights of the old things to continue.

Our Lord's commitment to rid us of old things is found in His statement, "Nor consider the things of old" (Is. 43:18). That idea stretches us and requires a quantum leap of faith. When something has been good and worked for us, how can we suddenly forget it? Straightway, we do not drink new wine because we assume the old is better. God has such confidence in Himself that He knows the new thing will eventually overtake us. He clobbers doubt. He silences fear by forecasting that He'll do the impossible.

The postmodern Church needs to starve her doubts and fears, and then feed her faith. Hearing the voice of God produces faith. Genesis 1 established the foundational principle of the walk of faith: *the evening and morning of a day!* Unless we are faced with *beginning in the evening* before advancing to the morning of God's new day, we'll never walk by faith. Starting in the dark prompts trusting God to guide.

The word of the Lord says, "Leave! I'll tell you where you are going once you get there!" This kind of blind faith requires total trust. After knowing the entirety of what God has done in Christ, why do we ever doubt Him? The apostle Peter says,

*Blessed be the God and Father of our Lord Jesus
Christ, who according to His abundant mercy has begot-
ten us again to a living hope through the resurrection
of Jesus Christ from the dead,*

*to an inheritance incorruptible and undefiled and
that does not fade away, reserved in heaven for you,*

*who are kept by the power of God through faith for
salvation ready to be revealed in the last time.*

1 Peter 1:3-5

If we can believe, all things are possible. Our God,
whose ways are past finding out, chooses to covenant with
what appears to be impossible. That's why God's forecast
says; "I will even make a road in the wilderness and rivers in
the desert." For us today, a road in the wilderness is no big
deal because of modern technology. When Isaiah was
prophesying almost three thousand years ago, this would
take an outstanding miracle. Who has heard of such a thing?
Possibility thinkers. God is infinite, and therefore impossible tasks do not limit Him. God is prepared to exceed our
highest thoughts and expectations. In every new wave of
glory, He exceeds all the previous things He has done.

Prophetically, there are many fresh desires in God's
heart for the Church. Elijah challenged backsliding Israel,
"How long will you falter between two opinions?" (1 Kings
18:21). Modern prophets must arise, follow his example,
and stir the Church to repentance in like manner. Prophets
are not spiritual fortunetellers but altar builders.

Elijah repaired the torn-down altar of Israel and illus-
trated her responsibility to it. The altar is the place of conviction, judgment, and resolve. We spiritually appraise
ourselves and not others. That judgment should be left to
God alone, who dwells in unapproachable light and therefore sees clearly the hearts of all human beings. At the altar
we stop courting the old order and finally enter into covenant with the new.

The Church can ill afford to *wobble* between the old and the new, failing to move in any specific direction. We must purpose to come on one side or the other, prophetically launching us to destiny's fulfillment. It is impossible to answer destiny's knock when we are double-minded and spiritually weakened by duality. Jesus was single-minded and set His face like flint to complete His assignment from the Father. The Church must come into the same quality of simplicity and singleness of mind. Look not at the old, which is passing into obsolescence, but look at the new, which is growing ever brighter with each passing day.

When we speak of *new* it can be translated as *fresh* also. Isaiah spoke of the assurance of salvation in Zion in Isaiah 62:2. Inclusive in this was a new, fresh name. What God is doing is so fresh that men are perplexed about what to call it. Usually, whatever we *name* we also *frame* into some controlling situation.

Whenever God does new things there are accompanying songs of praise. The blessed hallelujah psalm, Psalm 149, summons us to "sing to the Lord a new song." A fresh move demands a fresh song! Many times God will raise up someone to sing about what He is doing until we are disarmed of all of our defense mechanisms.

The prophet Jeremiah spoke of the intrinsic values of a new covenant. God brings a fresh emphasis on covenant whenever He does something fresh. Covenant is His vehicle to bring us into union with Christlikeness. During the process, we need the fresh mercies of Lamentations 3:22-23. Mercy is most appreciated when you are in the midst of uncertainty and not quite sure where this trip leads to. Sometimes you feel your life is a mess; yet God doesn't forsake you because of His plan for your life, which was well-conceived before the foundation of the world.

Finally, the prophet Ezekiel records a solemn oath of the Lord. He captures the mind of God in this wonderful insight: "I will give you a new heart and put a new spirit within you; I will take the heart of stone out of your flesh and give you a heart of flesh" (Ezek. 36:26).

The very thing that has been deceitful above all things and desperately wicked (see Jer. 17:9) is about to change because of the New Covenant. Before Christ our hearts could be cold, cruel, calculating, and conniving. He has transformed each heart into something special—soft, pliable, and mollified by the oil of the Holy Spirit. Whereas we used to listen to our heads to comprehend God, now we listen to our hearts. Scholarship is not necessarily the answer or the adversary. Let's take it and pair it with sensitive fellowship with the Holy Spirit.

There comes a season in every Christian's life when you can no longer trust your head (human understanding), but you must trust the God of your heart. In commending us to God, the wise sage of Proverbs says, "Trust in the Lord with all your heart, and lean not on your own understanding; in all your ways acknowledge Him, and He shall direct your paths" (Prov. 3:5-6).

Right now, because of the unpredictable nature of Kingdom operation, you will be troubled if you are leaning on your brain rather than His heart. Like the apostle John during the memorable last supper with Jesus, let's lean our heads upon His breast—His heart. We will either lean back into old order or lean into the new thing God has determined.

FAST-FORWARD INTO A NEW DAY

When I am watching a well-played football game on television, like many others, I dislike commercials, for they are an imposition. With the remote control, everything in me says, "Fast-forward!" Skip the mundane, the useless, and the unnecessary. Prophetically, the Church is in the same posture. It's time to close the container of old order and jettison into the new thing.

The release of God on the Day of Pentecost meant that the Church, as a fresh wineskin, had entered the fast lane into new things. The blast of God's breath broke every constriction and propelled them beyond any limitation. Their entire spiritual and mental paradigm changed dramatically. The fountains of their deep broke forth in a chorus of praise, decreeing new beginnings.

Webster defines *paradigm* as "a pattern, example, or model."[8] Christ is the pattern of things godly. No church, prayer group, or ministry can proclaim itself as the pattern. Each has missed the mark in some strategic point. Groups have decried others and made theirs the true preservers of the faith. However, time has proven them false—and how utterly futile this notion was to begin with. Christ was, is, and always will be God's pattern. In the words of the prophet Ezekiel, He is the house shown to the house of Israel (see Ezek. 43:10-12), and now to the Church. God's law, ordinances, designs, and arrangements are summed up in Christ. If the Church measures up to the pattern of new things, we will grow up into Christ the Head in His *current operation*. Prepare for the model of the Church to change drastically. This is not theory or propaganda—it's truth!

We are facing a spiritual ground zero—a word that pervaded American society since September 11, 2001. We likened the terrorists' attacks on the World Trade Center to the Japanese attack on Pearl Harbor on December 7, 1941. Many of our established structures are passing away with violence and a loud noise. It is a collective sound heard from coast to coast—from the White House to the State House, from the lowest hamlet to the most congested metropolis, and from the high court to the cathedral. The Holy Spirit is speaking things once considered spiritually unlawful. He is decoding what has been encoded into our spirit man. Like the astronomers during the early, pre-Reformation days, we must challenge scholastic and religious superstitions at the risk of being labeled heretics.

An illustration of this was Nicolas Copernicus proposing the sun, rather than the Earth, was the center of our solar system. Astronomers for many years refused to counter the Ptolemaic theory (Earth-centered solar system). Even if one thought differently, it was not to one's advantage to voice it. In later years, scholarship controlled by Romanism prevented many discoveries from being introduced. It's amazing the double shadow that religious death and faulty scholarship cast. For almost 14 centuries men embraced the wrong concept as truth. The Reformation and the Renaissance detonated a spiritual concussion with great synergy. It is still felt today.

God has elevated our spiritual horizons by declaring the Sonship of Christ in raising Him from the dead. (See Romans 1:4.) Christ was *declared*, which comes from the Greek word *horizo*, meaning, "to mark off by boundaries, determined."[9] It is fairly simple to see our English noun horizon is in the same word family as the verb *horizo*. The spirit of inquiry and exploration courses through our veins. It's a new phase of reformation. This time it is not to determine if the Earth is round or flat or to overthrow some religious despot. It is about possessing our full inheritance in Christ—discarding the old man and putting on the new.

By divine law, nothing happens in Earth until someone speaks it in the right timing of God. When all things are ready, the Heavens refuse to be silent. This is called *breakthrough*. Apostles and prophets of the Spirit are speaking on every continent. They are challenging us to pull up our stakes, lengthen our tent cords, and build new wineskins. Their words literally provoke a ground zero condition. It is the starting point and the most basic condition of the new order. So, whether we are speaking of Simon Peter preaching on the original Day of Pentecost or Luther, Calvin, or Wesley preaching in the early days of the Protestant Reformation, God releases the sound that changes everything. Let's fast-forward! Our destiny awaits us.

ENDNOTES

1. *Webster's II New College Dictionary*, "sound," 1054. (Boston, MA: Houghton Mifflin, 1999).

2. James Strong, "Greek Dictionary of the New Testament," *The New Strong's Exhaustive Concordance of the Bible* (Nashville: Thomas Nelson Publishers, 1984), # 869, # 852.

3. James Strong, "Greek Dictionary of the New Testament," *The New Strong's Complete Dictionary of Bible Words,* (Nashville: Thomas Nelson Publishers, 1996), #2279.

4. Adapted from David H. Stern, *Jewish New Testament Commentary* (Clarksville, MD: Jewish New Testament Publications, Inc., 1996), 219.

5. John R. Kohlenberger III, ed, *The Expanded Vine's* (Minneapolis, MN: Bethany House Publishers, 1984), 341.

6. Strong, "Greek Dictionary of the New Testament," *The New Strong's Exhaustive Concordance of the Bible*, #3661, #3674, #2372.

7. Ibid., #972, #970, #979.

8. *Webster's*, 979.

9. Kohlenberger, *The Expanded Vine's*, 274.

Chapter Two

THE CHURCH AND THE CURRENT REFORMATION

Now when these things had been thus prepared, the priests always went into the first part of the tabernacle, performing the services.

But into the second part the high priest went alone once a year, not without blood, which he offered for himself and for the people's sins committed in ignorance

the Holy Spirit indicating this, that the way into the Holiest of All was not yet made manifest while the first tabernacle was still standing.

It was symbolic for the present time in which both gifts and sacrifices are offered which cannot make him who performed the service perfect in regard to the conscience—

concerned only with foods and drinks, various washings, and fleshly ordinances imposed until the time of reformation.   Hebrews 9:6-10

It's essentially a temporary arrangement until a complete overhaul could be made. Hebrews 9:10b TM

...imposed until the coming of the new order.
                            Hebrews 9:10b TCNT

The year 1979 was a very earthshaking, transitional year for our ministry. Like a skilled master strategist, our Lord maneuvered our local church carefully through each step of the process to prepare us for this drastic change. Between 1975 and 1979, the Lord graced our ministry with apostolic teachers such as John Meares, Luther Blackwell,

and Paul Garlington. With their portions, they each mollified our local church wineskin, softening it with a greater
Kingdom understanding.

It all began by a fellow schoolteacher introducing me
to a young pastor in Richlands, North Carolina, in 1978.
This young man happened to be none other than my friend
and colleague, Kelley Varner. Pastor Varner had recently
moved from Maryland to Richlands to pioneer and pastor
Praise Tabernacle, a local church that would ultimately have
national and international influence. After hearing Pastor
Varner minister the Word of God, it was obvious that he
had something special for the local area. He reminded me
of Martin Luther's boldness and tenacity and John Calvin's
didactic skills, all in one package. In every sense of the word,
he was apostolic—illustrating the breakthrough predisposi-
tion accompanying apostolic ministry. He taught things
about the Kingdom of God few men in our local region
were even aware of. One of his most quoted passages of
Scripture was Proverbs 22:20-21:

> *Have I not written to you excellent things* [three-
> fold things] *of counsels and knowledge,*
> *That I may make you know the certainty of the
> words of truth, that you may answer words of truth to
> those who send to you?*

In his first published book, *Prevail–A Handbook for the
Overcomer*, Pastor Varner chronicled this principle of three-
fold things, as it is woven like a tapestry throughout the
Bible.

Not very long after coming to Richlands, he began a
radio broadcast, which he called *The Present Truth Bible
Hour*. Day after day Pastor Varner would teach Bible truths
that cut across the grain of religious thinking, shattering traditions without taking prisoners. I will never forget one particular series of teachings "Is the coming of the Lord any
minute or until?" This message sent shock waves throughout
the region. Everyone within a radius of one hundred miles

either loved Pastor Varner passionately or zealously persecuted him. It did not seem as though there were any fence-riders. Men polarized in one direction or the other. The truth was sharp, and it compelled everyone to make a quality decision. Thank God, things are different now!

During this same period, Pastor Varner began teaching a series of studies on the Tabernacle of Moses. I later came to understand that if a person understood the Tabernacle and the principles that governed its operations, one basically would have the keys to unlock the whole Bible. These classes were on Monday nights, so people who were thirsty and hungry were there. After more than 20 years, I would say these were probably some of the most insightful and impacting teachings I've ever witnessed. Lives were changed and traditions of men bombarded and battered. There was a keen awareness of the presence of God providing approbation to the gatherings. We wept, we laughed, we shouted and danced! Most of us were overjoyed that God would choose to open our eyes and reveal these sacred secrets to us.

The foundation of threefold things that was taught in those classes set the tone for much of how I have approached the Scriptures the last 23 years. It was very apparent we had come through two dimensions in God, and yet there was a third one. The church had been in temporary arrangements, but God was about to complete our journey. Once again, our theology was going through a complete overhaul. We could now put chapter and verse to the things God had prophetically spoken to us. Those impositions, such as traditional ideologies of eschatology and other fleshly ordinances, experienced an implosion. Many of our Pentecostal ways had become unnecessarily demanding and extremely unfair. God was launching us into the next phase of transition. This phase was not confined to one local church; it was regional in orientation. Little did we know God was *reforming the Church*!

THE BOOK OF HEBREWS

The Book of Hebrews has for a foundation the concept of *transition* or *crossing over. It is a book of reformation.* It was originally written to believers who were under pressure to return to Judaism because of severe persecution. Comparatively, men and women of God are under pressure today to maintain outdated wineskins that have served their purpose. Being warned against apostasy, Christians were encouraged to "go on unto perfection" (Heb. 6:1b KJV) or maturity. Scriptural documentation is used throughout the treatise to extol the virtues of the New Covenant. The Scriptures prove conclusively that the sacrifice and covenant of Christ perfectly fulfilled the messianic promises, and that the old dispensation had failed miserably.

This epistle was one of comparison and contrast, showing someone who may be reading with a Levitical bent the splendor of Christ versus the fading glory of the Temple system and its ineffectual sacrifices. The key word throughout the epistle is better! As one studies this wonderful epistle and distills the truths in it, every thought builds a classic case for reformation theology.

With this as a backdrop, the Lord decrees a *time of reformation. Time* is again the Greek word *kairos*, which means that this season is *specific, instant* intervention, not a space of intervention. *Reformation* is translated from the Greek word *diorthosis*, which means "to straighten thoroughly, rectification." Reformation is activity that causes something to rise perpendicularly, to be erect, straight, and upright.[1] The general idea is the right ordering or arrangement of things, a total restoration or an amendment when the imperfect must be superseded by something better.

In most cultures and subcultures, reformation makes better by removing faults and defects. In the Kingdom ecosystem, it is a Christological corrective, reforming with truth what has become deformed by superstition and traditions of men. As a basic concept in chemistry, reformation means, "to heat...under pressure, with or without a catalyst, to produce cracking and a greater yield."[2] God cracked the earth suit of Jesus on the cross of Calvary. Out of Him came the Christ to be corporately reproduced into a many-membered son. When God cracked Jesus, He cracked Adam! From this came the desire of God's heart when He said, "Let Us make man in Our image" (Gen. 1:26a). It took the heat and pressure of the Cross, the central focus of human history, to reform Adam, who had become severely deformed.

WHY ANOTHER PHASE OF REFORMATION?

The current Church order and institution limits and prevents the possibility of Kingdom advancement to its fullness. Every move of God, exempting none, has thus far seen and experienced the Lord in part. The keynote address in the Book of Acts was and is *the Kingdom of God.* (Read Acts 1:6-8; 2:36; 3:19-26; 5:42; 8:12-13,35; 14:21-22; 17:2-3; 20:25-27; 28:23, 30-31.) A priority in preaching the Kingdom of God is on declaring the Lordship of Jesus Christ. God's Kingdom is His ecosystem, which is conducive to life for Himself and mankind. Placed into a hostile environment to both, this present cosmos, His Kingdom is still able to manifest and reproduce itself. The apostles preached the Kingdom as a present reality with future intentions. The first message, which means priority, Jesus preached was on the Kingdom of God (See Matthew 4:17.)

Herein lies the cause for reformation: God's Kingdom, not man's, must be declared, not denied, and established in divine order. This order allows every man to know God intimately, respect the collegiality of brethren, and honor the uniqueness of individual function. Until divine intervention, there is no dynamic intact to expose disorder, which is the various methods of control utilized today. The current Church system is a composite of this. Reformation exposes the beastly vindictiveness of the religious system that has become an entrenched institution of protectionism. Religion is an over-worked machine driven by *profit-making* rather than *prophet-making*! In many ways, it compares to the same system Jesus faced in His day, a system that had very little compassion for the wounded, broken, and hurting. It was more about the influx of mammon. (See Luke 16:14-15.)

The emerging Church of the current reformation must break out of the vacuum and cast off the shackles of history's web and culture's dough, thus releasing a greater expression of Christ's total victory over the four universal horns: sin, sickness, poverty, and death. The spirit realm, nature, and history demand that a vacuum be filled. The Bible states that a clean house must be filled once an evil spirit has been cast out, or it will come back seeking habitation with a more intensified force. (See Luke 11:24-26.) Anyone acquainted with farming understands you cannot leave a field uninhabited; it will automatically cover with weeds and other unsatisfactory vegetation.

History will always be filled with the story of someone or something new and interesting; it simply is. Its web is another story! It is the tapestry spun by out-of-order systems of men, trapping God's people into ideologies that rob them of abundant life. Part of history is the stories of people with great negative influence. They lead others in a detrimental direction.

Conversely, God's desire is that spiritual leaders lead His people into His-Story. God's story is a systematic accounting, a continuous methodical record in order and time, of some of the important things God has done. It's called the Bible. No one book contains a record of everything God has done. Secular man has produced historians who have chronicled public events shaping human behavior. What the modern Church must decide is whether God's story, with no additions, or man's web is written in our best interest?

Culture's dough is another question! Most dictionaries define culture as the training and refinement of mind, tastes, and manners; the intellectual side of things that produces preferences and not necessarily rock-solid convictions.

Something is conspicuously absent in this listing: the training of man's spirit to be sensitive and discerning of the Lord's voice. Because of preference, six worship styles have evolved out of culture's dough as dominant. They each add unique distinctions and contributions to the picture we call modern Christianity. These worship styles include:

- The Evangelical Church: primarily focuses on getting people saved and training them through Church schools
- The Bible Expository Church: teaching people the Word of God
- The Body Life Church: helping people find fulfillment and meaning through significant relationships
- The Liturgical Church: magnifying God in atmospheric worship
- The Congregation Church: involving members and expecting participation in the local body of Christ
- The Holiness/Pentecostal/Charismatic Church: emphasis is upon the baptism of the Holy Spirit, the gifts of the Spirit, and fruit of the Spirit

No matter what our personal preference may be, it is imperative to respect the other flavors. No single expression has encountered or experienced all of God's glory. God has used each model to achieve portions of His higher goal. The goal of every leadership paradigm should be to teach God's sheep to hear His voice. If leaders accomplish that particular priority, they have excelled in leadership and fulfilled what true biblical leadership is all about. Leaders must lead people to the Lord, the source of life, and not to themselves, who are only containers of the source.

If we only hear God or drink from the cup of one distinctive, we will miss much of the Lord's manifestation of Himself. Sometimes, to our own amazement, the Lord still has many expressions to His one flock. All sheep don't look alike or behave alike! We are uniquely different, and therefore flock into diverse folds. What is mandatory from God is that we respect and affirm one another as belonging to the Lord.

In reformation, the Lord starts to crack the existing wineskins. This is neither pleasant, nor necessarily gratifying work to the vessel used of God in this task. God jars the old wineskins violently, producing a threefold reaction in the religious leadership and the people:

1. They are filled with wrath. (See Luke 4:18-21; 28-30.)
2. Divisions are forced—some people see the need for cracking the old. (See John 7:40-44; 9:16; 10:19.)
3. Leadership will plot to kill the wineskin cracker. (See John 11:49-53.)

You see, if the old wineskins aren't discarded, the volatility and combustibility of the new wine will destroy the old skin. Wisdom teaches one can never place new wine into old skins. I am amazed at our tendency to maintain the fortress of present activity in God without enlarging our tents of expectation for years. We will drink the same wine from the same wine cup and never discern the wine has become unbearable. Much is done to keep the cup intact. To move us out of this lull, God raises up a reformer with the dynamic of frustration with the old, who refuses to quit until something has changed in the old way of conducting business.

Jesus was just this type of reformer. He cracked the wineskin of the synagogue, probably constructed while the people were in Babylonian captivity. Synagogues produced a *centralized concept* of worship that led to monotheistic religiosity. In John 4, Jesus declared He was decentralizing their worship concepts because the Father was looking for reality in their worship. A casual look at the synagogue will reveal that the Church adopted much of its operational approach once they left home meetings as their primary gathering place.

> The basic sense of *synagoge* is that of bringing together or assembling (cf. a gathering of people, a collection of books or letters, the ingathering of harvest, the mustering of

troops, the knitting of brows, the drawing in of a sail, and in logic the deduction or demonstration).

In larger cities there were many synagogues. Like modern local churches, they were always self-supporting. Congregations were responsible. The names of donors were inscribed on parts of the building that they would endow, and sometimes endowments were very large.

Synagogues were built on the high point of a town, thus conveying the highest position in the minds of the people. Most synagogues were built with the entrance facing Jerusalem. The ark with the law is at the entrance so that the people may face it too. Each synagogue had scrolls of the Old Testament. A podium with a reading desk was there. Other articles include lamps, trumpets, seats, and vessels for washing. Paintings are found in the form of mosaics or murals.[3]

The congregation was divided, men on one side, women on the other, a low partition, five or six feet high, running between them. Synagogues were places of reading, teaching, preaching, prayer, and almsgiving.[4]

In purely Jewish communities, a board of seven handled the community affairs, in mixed communities, or where there is more than one synagogue, a board of three. The officers are the servant and the president. Presidents were highly regarded and were often members of the board. They would preside at worship, and see to the erection and care of the building. Presidents were elected for a term and may be reelected. The office often remained in the same family. To be excommunicated from the synagogue was a barring from entry into the building or meeting, nor merely exclusion from the local community, but expulsion from national fellowship.[5]

It is fairly easy to see that most Protestant systems are either direct descendants of the synagogue or slight abbreviations. These systems do not necessarily lend to an atmosphere welcoming the presence of the Lord. Lacking in passion, the overmastering zeal and enthusiasm for the Lord is not present in the leadership or people. He is not the aim or the object pursued with zeal. High ideals such as "fervent in spirit" and "doing things heartily as unto the Lord" are conspicuously absent.

The primary way Jesus chose to crack the existing wineskin was *inclusiveness*. He dealt with the chronological prejudice—Jesus called little children and blessed them. (See Mark 10:13-16; 9:14-32.) Jesus really jarred the wineskin with racial inclusiveness—He ministered to Samaritans as well as Jews (See John 4; see also Matthew 15:21-28.) God also cracks our wineskins by redefining our Church growth concepts—He is bringing many colors, cultures, and kinds together. This blows apart the homogeneous paradigm and creates a more consistent mind-set with true Kingdom culture. Respecting the faith of women, Jesus dealt with gender prejudice, giving women their rightful place as sons. (See Galatians 3:28.) The Book of Job deals with God raising daughters to the levels of sons and rightful heirs. (See John 1:12 and Job 42:12-15.)

NEW CLASS OF MEN ON EARTH

Reformation always creates a new quality, condition, or class of men on the Earth. The Holy Spirit actively prepares a new generation to carry the torch of Kingdom advancement into a new era at a higher level. Reformation allows the Christian culture and influence to destroy the power of unbridled and unrestrained society, primarily dominated by fierce individualism and anarchy. A prime example of this point is when Israel entered the Promised Land, inhabited by giants, with an order to dispossess the giants and establish a people who understood themselves to be a peculiar people, a holy nation, and a Kingdom of priests. Israel, like the New Covenant citizen, was to be a new creature.

Using the Tabernacle of Moses as a model, God established a systematic order to reformation truth. (See

Proverbs 22:20-21; Deuteronomy 16:16; Exodus 23:14; Luke 13:32.) In each case, the focal point of God's movement did not remain with the same people-group all the time. God is far vaster than that, and certainly more multidimensional in His thinking. Unfortunately, the new wave people are met with harsh persecution from the former move of God. An example of this is when the Catholics and the Lutheran Protestants shamefully pursued the Anabaptists and subjected them to torturous murders. In postmodern reformation, the established Church and probably all her flavors will become the new persecutors if she doesn't catch the wind currents of reformation.

Historically, from about 1517 or the early sixteenth century until the beginning of the early1900s or twentieth century God reformed the outer court of the Tabernacle of Moses, consisting of the brazen altar and the laver. Because of the prolonged darkness of Romanism, it took almost four hundred years to reform the outer court. When anything is being recovered after many years of being lost, it requires sanctified effort to launch a new beginning.

- Martin Luther preached *justification by faith*. Jesus was revealed as the Savior, Justifier, Healer and Finisher. The reality of the new birth and the Feast of Passover was correctly restored (brazen altar).
- The Anabaptists, John Wesley, and The Holiness Movement. There's a restoration of the truth of water baptism in the name of the Lord as well as sanctification. The New Covenant is sealed and Jesus, as Baptizer and Sanctifier, is experienced (brazen laver).

The opening of the twentieth century was the time God began to reform the holy place and all the furniture of the Christian experience within it. The holy place in the Tabernacle of Moses parallels the Feast of Pentecost. The furniture of the holy place—the candlestick, the Table of

Shewbread, and the Altar of Incense—is a type of the practices of the Acts Church. (See Acts 2:42.) Time was significantly reduced; in fact, it was cut down to about one-fourth of the previous reformation period. Each level brought radical opposition to a system that merchandised God's people. Aggressive self-denial promoted a holy passion that promoted reformation and helped it to escalate.

- Charles Parham, William Seymour, Evan Roberts, Azusa Street, and Wales. There was a rebirth of Pentecostal fire and experience. The Holy Spirit baptism produced the fruit and the gifts of the Spirit, along with spiritual ministry. It was a true Feast of Pentecost and Jesus, the Light of the World, was revealed (The Apostles' Doctrine—candlestick).

- Canada and USA—(1948-55). There was a renewed understanding of the *fivefold ministry*, Body-of-Christ life and ministry. The Holy Spirit emphasized the *laying on of hands* and *covenant commitment*. Jesus, the Bread of Life and Living Word, was revealed (the table of shewbread).

- The late 1950s and 1960s—teachings on the Tabernacle of David. (See Acts 15:13-18; Amos 9:11-12.) This was a post-World War II move of God running simultaneously with the introduction of the modern nuclear age of militarism. The Holy Spirit emphasized *praying in the Spirit* and *worship in New Testament order*. Jesus, the Mediator and High Priest, was revealed (the golden altar of incense).

- The 1970s through 1990s—moved experientially beyond a rent veil. (See Hebrews 10:19-24.) It is the transition of moving from the Feast of Pentecost to the Feast of Tabernacles. There is access into *biblical maturity—expressing full sonship and priesthood.* Jesus, the Word made flesh, is manifested (the veil).

The Church of the twenty-first century must be reformed in the practical realities of the Most Holy Place. (See Revelation 4.) This will unfold in many key areas. Dispensationally, the Kingdom of God is at hand—within grasp of those who have pressed on to knowing the Lord. Because our message and experience must always be Christ-centered, Jesus the Lord, the Overcomer, the Head of the Church, and the Fullness of the Godhead bodily is magnified. Stepping through a rent veil, the Church transitions from anointing to glory, partaking of Christ's throne as the overcoming Church. What Church polity thought to be heresy—teachings on full, mature sonship and total adoption—becomes the norm. Experientially, an overcoming Church is caught up to God and His throne, the redemption of the mortal body occurs, and a company rules with Jesus Christ (the Ark of the Covenant and His mercy seat).

THREE ESSENTIAL REALITIES

In every phase of reformation, there are three distinct yet correlated releases when God is reforming the Church and culture. There is a release in *technology*, enhancing and advancing communication techniques and abilities. There is a *teaching* unique to the *times of transition.* There is a *transposition musically,* and a *unique sound* of the Heavens is expressed uninhibitedly. Each is consistent with this principle: *When nature is ready to reveal a thing, it cannot be hidden! Likewise, when the Heavens are ready to reveal a thing, nothing on Earth can stop it either!* (See Galatians 4:4-5; Daniel 9:1-2.)

Note this brief chronology of the three reformation tools—music, technology, and a new message:

- Luther and the Wesleys gave us *hymns*—music.
- The reformation of Pentecost gave us *spiritual songs* (early Pentecostals) and *psalms* (Charismatic Movement)—music.

- Gutenberg gave us the *printing press* in the early stages of the pre-Reformation (1455 A.D.). This movable-type printing press produced the Bible—technology.

- The reformation of Pentecost was preceded by the *telephone, tape recorder,* and the invention of the *light bulb*—technology.

- The 1940s and 1950s gave us greater usage of *television* as a medium of communication after Farnsworth demonstrated a working model of a television in 1927—technology.

- The 1960s began the evolution of *computer technology* after the first electronic computer was built in 1945—technology.

- The late 1990s gave us the *Internet* and a *global superhighway* in everyday life after the *Internet* (ARPA) went online in 1969—technology.

- The outer court was reformed with the messages of *justification by faith, teachings on water baptism,* and *sanctification* experientially through spiritual disciplines—message.

- The Holy Place was reformed with the messages of the *baptism of the Holy Spirit* and the entire corresponding *spiritual ministry*—message.

- The Holy of Holies must be reformed with the message of the *finished work* and the understanding and application of *His total triumph over sin, sickness, poverty,* and *death*—message.

SHIFTING OF CONSCIOUSNESS

The natural sign of the *global superhighway of Internet communication* speaks prophetically to the times of God's release from the Heavens. God's Church must learn to discern the times more adeptly just as meteorologists discern the weather patterns more skillfully today. Technology has permitted us to connect globally in a matter of seconds. It is first the natural then the spiritual. The Church must become global in her thinking! Yes, we must have our Jerusalem, Judea, and Samaria. However, the large picture consists of the nations of the Earth. Can we move beyond our stifling, crippling issues—such as gender prejudice, racial intolerance, and denominational walls—and elevate the nations into the reality of God? Our small thinking has hindered the spread of the Gospel—the good news of Christ's victory over death and its cohorts. God's heart is for all men in all places.

As the vehicle of the Kingdom of God, the global Church has become the *network* of King Jesus to reach the harvest of the nations. (See Matthew 13:47.) Some of His servants are *great casters* of the net. (See Matthew 4:18-20.) This is the apostolic thrust from the Book of Acts until the current time. Others are *great menders* and *washers* of the net. (See Matthew 4:21-22; Luke 5:1-2.) These are your reformers! Pair the two together and the Kingdom net functions properly.

KINGDOM NETWORKING

Networking is one of the new, cutting-edge wineskins being used by God to contain and release this distilled wine of reformation. Certainly, it is not the only modern wineskin appropriated of God to touch this generation. However, it is a viable means to connect ministries together without aggressive forms of manipulation and control devices, which eventually produce denominationalism. Because of valid concerns, some God-fearing brethren think that networking is no more than a modern high-tech term for denominationalism. It is vital to alleviate this notion because God wants brethren partnering as associates, understanding the true spirit by which networking relationships should be entered.

Networking is the interconnecting and the interrelating of mobile ministers and autonomous local churches through covenant participation. Barnabas and Paul, along with Peter, John, and James, networked together for the purpose of the Kingdom. (See Galatians 2:8-10.) It is the development of an extended community of ministries committed to further God's prudent purposes, which is His Kingdom. Networking is the sharing and exchanging of our lives in such a manner that it interlocks us together willingly. As with all New Testament relationships, it is something recognized on the basis of divine appointment. These relationships are never forced or coerced.

Essential to networking are elements such as accountability, vision, and destiny. Network partners realize their destinies are locked and tied into each other. These properly link a network together, thus establishing a suitable structure for extending the Kingdom of God in all the Earth. When operated correctly, no individual ministry loses its specific identity or fingerprint of mission and autonomy because of joint participation. Great value is placed upon concepts of family and covenant relationships earmarked by the joining of hearts.

NEW APOSTOLIC LEADERS

Because of the nature of the apostolic ministry, apostolic persons will lead most networks. Again, this speaks to function rather than hierarchical importance. *Apostolic* denotes "sent"![6] It is an official mission. Anytime God is doing something new or fresh it is first and foremost apostolic. The apostles of the first century were wonderful models of the networking ideal. So, networking is not a new idea in the strictest sense of the word. In a time of reformation, it is something fresh for most independent ministries. When a thing is apostolic in nature, the seed, the grace, and the sustained anointing for new realms of the Spirit are within its ranks. Many brethren agree that this word and work has special breakthrough potential. When the New Covenant dispensation was launched, it commenced with apostles. They were the initial foundational aids in God's new Kingdom ecosystem. Without apostles *first*, there is no official channel to release God's purposes. (See First Corinthians

12:28.) Apostles are the embodiments of God's heart, vision, and destiny as something new begins.

History has given many records of the networking idea as various leaders have tried to implement it unsuccessfully. Among other things, the Protestant Reformation produced a number of networks that ultimately became denominations. In most cases, the initial intent was not denominational in spirit. Most servant-leaders earnestly desired to correct the old Roman Catholic wineskin. Much to their anguish, they were excommunicated and had to seek other relational involvements.

Running concurrent to the Protestant Reformation, Charles V (1500-1558), the powerful Emperor of Germany and King of Spain, attempted to establish the European nations into a free community of equal partners as well. This was apostolic in every sense of the word and a highly visible networking effort. His aim was to create an alliance of peoples who, while retaining their own sovereignty, would be linked together by a united Church and common desire for European unity. His goal was to thwart insurgent German Protestantism. Although only a seedling, this was a geopolitical maneuver that did not succeed because of the impure motives of carnal men's hearts. It did, however, cement the idea that the Church would be instrumental in defining the culture of late medieval Europe.

That seed planted in the early sixteenth century has now matured. It is the European Union, which is a network of nations in alliance for the common good of modern Europe. If carnal human beings realize the value of networking, why shouldn't the Church? Even though there are national and cultural distinctions among partners, they have made these secondary and entered into a networking relationship. They have settled the fact that many can accomplish much more than one in a global market and society. The format is such that participation is voluntary and relational rather than forced. Rational men comprehend that great strength comes when we compound together exponentially.

CORE VALUE SYSTEM

As with any networking relationship, there were some very specific conditions each member agreed to before they were accepted into the European Union. These conditions are the *core values* of the network. Core values are the most important, central, or innermost part of a value system. Stated or not, every community or network has a core value system. As to the current paradigm of God, He is raising an army of priests forming a Melchisedec priesthood. These men and women are being mobilized into a great strategic command. Covenant, biblical models of servant-leadership, spiritual maturity, balanced exercise of authority, love for all nations, ethnic and gender diversity, and a balance between biblical orthodoxy and praxis will best characterize this army.

Establishing a network solves the dilemma of "man being alone." Networks create a shared identity for many to connect with and find a sense of security. When you consider that security, self-worth, and significance are three essentials for man's well being, then it is much easier to appreciate the truth of networking. It is a *vehicle*, not a *box*, for those who interlock themselves to become both transparent and accessible to one another. As networks are established, brethren are strengthened and our flow in God increases by amassing mutual supporters and creating teamwork. We must appreciate God's strategy behind networking: He is fostering and developing a team of ministries with the same objectives. Remember, great teams—not great individuals—win championships.

The network community freely acknowledges Christ as the Head of the community, with His headship being implemented through a leadership team. The team has been broken and purged of wrong motivations by the fires of the Holy Spirit. Because of diversity in gifting, a representative apostle will emerge as Simon Peter did, with a necessary leadership focus, but not as a lord over God's heritage.

Within the community, this person becomes a channel of release, causing the desire of Heaven to be imported into the Earth. The network community is authorized and given spheres or measures of influence in which Kingdom and non-Kingdom activities are loosed and bound. Also, the leadership team identifies corporate philosophy and core values within the operating system of the network structure.

Beyond the network leadership team, there are other valid apostles, prophets, and ministers within the network. Different ministries have different philosophies that must be embraced and encouraged. According to the apostle Paul, these are gifts given by the same Spirit. (See First Corinthians 12:4.) It is unreasonable to think all apostles and prophets within a network will have the same ministry unction or directive; however, the network must recognize, appreciate, and be inclusive of the different measures. (See Second Corinthians 10:12-16.)

Every network must have as its main priority the propagation of the Kingdom of God. That is what binds the network together. All related ministries will have their portion of empowering gifts. Wise leaders provide outlets for these ministries to come forth for the mutual benefit of the network. With the collective functionality of all, the network fulfills its calling. Fresh anointing is given by God to make sure there is fresh strength to finish the network assignment. While respect and great value is placed upon diversity, every network must have as its main aim God's call, His mission and objective, and yet be open to all other administrations and operations within the network and other networks.

PROPHETIC PARTNERS

Prophetic partners are extremely significant to any apostolic network. Inherent within the office of the prophet is the God-given ability to assist people in learning how to hear the voice of God. Once Christians can hear clearly the voice of God for themselves, they have no further need for personal prophets. New Testament prophets are ordained to aid in the unveiling of God's present-day purposes. Along with apostles, they are appointed over nations and over Kingdom spheres to determine what activities are permitted in them. (See Jeremiah 1:10.) The prophetic river flowing out of them because all may prophesy doesn't necessarily define prophets! The greatest evidence to a New Testament prophetic function of the Ephesians 4:11 order is when people under their ministry can practically discern and clearly hear the voice of the Lord for themselves.

With world events occurring the way they are, God is providing a platform for national prophets to emerge and be heard. At this level, prophets provide wisdom, counsel, and instruction to governments and republics. This authority is given to keep the integrity of the heart of God fresh within the decision-making quarters of that nation. As with Elijah, modern prophets will be restored to a place of respectability even in secular circles. Prophets of this level engender a healthy respect in their appearing. (See First Samuel 16:4.) Their words precipitate life and death, blessing and cursing. Leaders will ask, "Do you come peaceably?" In some developing nations around the world, this has already begun to transpire with things such as diplomatic recognition and leaders seeking a fresh word from God. The Word of God flowing freely from the lips of prophets is echoing throughout legislative rooms and capital buildings. Within the concept of a network, prophets will never be standing alone against hundreds. Their real strength will lie in their connection with network partners.

NETWORK PHILOSOPHY

Every previous move of God's Spirit has been named, tagged, framed, and managed into a denominational device by well-intentioned men of God. How do we, the twenty-first century Church, prevent networking from becoming such a device? The key is within the philosophy of the network. Networking doesn't have to become one more imperialistic hammer that segregates God's people into sectarian splinters through pounding some revelatory distinctive. All networks must respect fellow networks as equally called of God. There is a wonderful Kingdom opportunity to build with, not against, brethren. In fact, the very function of the word *networking* almost always suggests diversified inclusiveness.

God has released something fresh and new from the Heavens. Godly servants are focused on finishing the assignment of the Lord with new foresight. True networks with the Kingdom spirit of networking are becoming empowerment agencies, assisting men and women of God as they complete their God-appointed assignments. Thomas Fuller captures the biblical sense of empowerment in this splendid thought: "If you have knowledge, let others light their candles by it."[7]

Network leaders must choose to fan the flames of refreshing fire in the lives of all God places within their sphere of influence. Our mandate is to light candles, not to blow them up or out. This requires a spirit of facilitation, not management. The tendency has always been for men to manage the move of God's Spirit in the Earth rather than allowing Him to move, thus placing handcuffs on the movement.

Should we dare think spiritual and mental adjustments are needed in order to maintain a proper network philosophy? After years of watching men abuse people and power, I must answer with an emphatic yes! For instance, traditional leadership structures lead to domination and worldly management styles. In the Kingdom of God, this must cease.

The world always places traditional hierarchical leadership at the top of a pyramid design. Then the focus is on the leadership, as everyone becomes inept, looking to him or her. This system begets mediocrity and complacency and thwarts the spirit of initiative in most members. The life and vitality of this design always moves upward in direction. There should be no startling surprises by the impending, disastrous results. It creates a social pecking order with no one desiring to be at the bottom of the pyramid. People within this kind of network structure become used, unnoticed, and barely paid token appreciation, if any at all. Thus, an attention deficit is created, breeding a system of competition and sibling rivalry.

Historically, denominationalism has produced this type of model. The so-called unsung, unimportant people are only necessary to keep the structure intact or build the network numerically. How does the modern Church change this?

A pristine understanding of Ephesians 2:20 gives a definitive answer. Apostles are truly at the bottom of the building rather than the top. No Bible apostle is over anyone! They supply energy and vitality that flows upward into the rest of the network. In humility they de-emphasize themselves and nurture the unsung heroes and heroines who were previously despised and forgotten. As facilitators, they follow the admonition of Paul.

> *Don't push your way to the front; don't sweet-talk your way to the top. Put yourself aside, and help others get ahead. Don't be obsessed with getting your own advantage. Forget yourselves long enough to lend a helping hand.* Philippians 2:3-4 TM

The idea is to be other-people-centered. Leaders must be intentional in their efforts to make room for, serve, and support others within the network organism. In the current Western Christian enterprise, this is a very different approach, to say the least. Nevertheless, the Church has a very important decision to make: Do we want something relevant to our times, or something obsolete and structurally inaccurate? What is relevant produces *freedom*; what is irrelevant produces *imposition*.

The writer of the Epistle to the Hebrews spoke of things imposed until a *time of reformation*. (See Hebrews 9:10.) The normal Church leadership design is basically obsolete and in great need of reformation. Attitudinally, human beings are driven by power rather than service. In most church operations, power will center in a person rather than a team. This becomes the seedbed for corruption if that person doesn't learn to delegate his authority to other trustworthy people. In the priesthood of all believers, a Melchisedec Order, this is not so. This Order is essentially a saints' movement born of the spirit of empowerment. The saints are secured and empowered because their leaders are secured and empowered. Subsequently, a Joshua Generation is mobilized from this secured state. The saints find themselves perched upon destiny's doorstep. Our full inheritance in Christ is just before us. The time has come to go up at once and take the land without fail.

Powerful network mobilization will happen because of a conscious choice to empower all related ministers and ministries within the network. When leaders follow Paul's admonition in Philippians 2:3-4, there is a clear shift to people power. The heart of God is beautifully portrayed, capturing the true functionality of New Testament leadership. In military jargon, mobilization is placing our forces before the enemy in strategic detail. At this point, leadership becomes tactical. There's a responsibility incumbent to arrange the network forces in such a manner that God's wisdom is clearly revealed.

Through mobilization we emphatically declare ourselves to be God's Army. (See Ephesians 6:10-18 and Revelation 19:11-16.) Part of the Church's calling is to be an army. Networking fully equips us through diversified impartation to function as that army. Partaking of the wisdom, knowledge, talents, and strengths of many is much better than the burden of equipping the saints being on a few superstars. God's army has to be prepared for spiritual combat and occupation. We must contend to see the nations removed from the demoniacal domination of the gods of this cosmos. And, we must care for the harvest as God brings it in. Networking offers the opportunity for God's army to be thoroughly responsible. The ability to be responsible is one of the many trademarks of spiritual maturity.

COVENANTAL CONNECTIONS

God is a God of covenant! No one and no thing can refute this truth. Covenant is a matter of the heart and not the head. Throughout the Bible, we read of men and women with whom God has cut covenant. The names Adam, Noah, Abraham, Sarah, Moses, David, Hannah, and Jesus are just a few that immediately come to mind. In fact, the Bible is divided into two major divisions—the Old Covenant and the New Covenant.

It is proper to conclude, then, that God's people are to be covenant people as they express their sonship in this Earth. Living a lifestyle outside of the bonds of covenant was unacceptable and almost unimaginable behavior among the early Church. (See Acts 2:40-47; 4:32-35.) The times pressed them to become involved with each other on a daily basis. Perhaps a key study in the New Testament is all the truth spinning out of references to "one another." This is why networks must choose covenantal relationships as their core emphasis. It is highly impossible and impractical to think of fulfilling our destiny without becoming a covenantal community.

Community implies "having things in common." *Webster's Dictionary* defines *community* as "a group of people living together as a smaller social unit within a larger one, and having interests, work, etc. in common."[8] From this derives ideas such as community centers, community properties, community chest, and on a larger scale, community colleges. There is an acknowledgment that we are divinely assigned to be "bone of bone" (see Gen. 2:23) to each other in community. That in itself makes us community, which produces certain fluidity. Our dreams, hopes, aspirations, priorities and commitments constrain us to reinforce a common set of values and goals. Our consciousness, then, becomes corporate and not individualistic. In networking, it is imperative to understand we are related by blood (the blood of the Lamb), water (the water of His Word), and Spirit. Covenant demands that we educate ourselves concerning relationships.

No covenant works without properly focused relationships that are willfully entered into. In covenant, brethren choose to abide together in peace and harmony as unto the Lord.

Jesus proclaimed one of the greatest maxims of truth concerning covenant in this statement: "Therefore what God has joined together, let not man separate" (Mt. 19:6b). The focus is on *what* God has joined and not *whom* God has joined. *What* is indispensable and *who* is not. *What* depicts corporate destiny, corporate purpose, and a principle of life together. *Whats* are appointments made in Heaven that we must awaken to in Earth. These appointments are assignments made before the foundation of the world. They have nothing to do with class, color, or culture.

When God joins or yokes together people with a purpose, *nothing* of man must be allowed to separate them. The main idea of *joined* or *yoked* is to "couple together with a sense of each completing the other."[9] Certain men and women that I am joined to help to complete me. There is no break in continuity, any empty expanse, vacancy, chasm, or parting of company when we are yoked together. It is reasonable to note that every marriage and ministry connection is not necessarily God joining that situation together. God does not join the ox (ox nature = Christ nature) and the donkey (wild ass nature = Ishmael nature) together. (See Deuteronomy 22:10.)

Barnabas and Saul were a networking team that God joined together. They allowed circumstances to put them asunder. It behooves us to learn from their example. (See Romans 15:4; First Corinthians 10:11.) Their story begins like this: Barnabas, a man of reputation, introduces Saul to the brethren. (See Acts 9:26-27.) Later Barnabas is commissioned to go to Antioch. (See Acts 11:23-26.) The Holy Spirit separates Barnabas and Saul, prophets and teachers, unto the apostolic ministry. (See Acts 13:1-3, 5.) Saul becomes the chief speaker as the team functions extra-locally. (See Acts 14:12-14.) God's order was still Barnabas and Saul. Saul becomes Paul, and Barnabas and Paul appear with other significant leadership at the Jerusalem Council. (See Acts 15:22-25.) Once the Council is adjourned, Barnabas and Paul remain a tandem bearing the epistle derived out of the corporate anointing of the Council. (See Acts 15:30-35.)

Eventually, they allowed great contention to separate them. (See Acts 15:36-40.) Many have stated that the reason for this separation was to properly birth God's order of apostles and prophets as teammates. Regardless of the reason, these two great apostles allowed personal opinions to separate *what* God had joined together. In Acts 15:39, the Greek word translated "contention" is *paroxusmos*, which is where we get the word *paroxysm*, "a sudden outburst as of laughter, rage, or sneezing; fit; spasm."[10] In this instance, Paul literally was having a fit about taking John Mark with them on the next mission. This was typical of Paul's choleric temperament, which always had to be in charge. When he was older, we see a marked change in the later writings of Philemon 9 and Second Timothy 4:11. In lonely imprisonment, rejected by many, this ambassador of reconciliation understands the value of a covenant he broke many years earlier and is willing to do something about it.

Covenant means stepping beyond our individuality into corporate greatness, a greatness that is greater than anything we could accomplish alone. To live a challenging, worthwhile, and productive life, a son of God must be a part of something that is greater than he is. We are all unique with many points of difference that distinguish us one from another. Every person brings all of this into the presence of the Father and into a networking relationship, to be interwoven by love, faith, and hope in Jesus Christ. In the process of weaving this corporate tapestry, we also have many opportunities to portray the nature of Christ. The thread that continually surfaces in this tapestry is that of committed interpersonal relationships. When we maintain basic ethics, which is simply a system of moral standards or values, relationships work properly. A few of these ethics are as follows:

The command we have from Christ is blunt: Loving God includes loving people. You've got to love both.
1 John 4:21 TM

Love from the center of who you are; don't fake it. Run for dear life from evil; hold on for dear life to good. Be good friends who love deeply; practice playing second fiddle. Romans 12:9-10 TM

Help needy Christians; be inventive in hospitality. Bless your enemies; no cursing under your breath. Laugh with your happy friends when they're happy; share tears when they're down. Get along with each other; don't be stuck-up. Make friends with nobodies; don't be the great somebody. Romans 12:13-16 TM

Stay on good terms with each other, held together by love. Hebrews 13:1 TM

Post this at all the intersections, dear friends: Lead with your ears, follow up with your tongue, and let anger straggle along in the rear. James 1:19 TM

Everything that goes into a life of pleasing God has been miraculously given to us by getting to know, personally and intimately, the One who invited us to God. The best invitation we ever received! We were also given absolutely terrific promises to pass on to you—your tickets to participation in the life of God after you turned your back on a world corrupted by lust.
2 Peter 1:3-4 TM

Friends come and friends go, but a true friend sticks by you like family. Proverbs 18:24 TM

Guard your tongue from profanity, and no more lying through your teeth. Turn your back on sin; do something good. Embrace peace—don't let it get away!
Psalm 34:13-14 TM

These Christlike ethics are essential in networking because a network is a multicultural and a multiethnic unit. Comparatively, like fishing nets, individual strings are tied and knotted together. Unity, like the precious anointing oil, is always diverse. Each part that helps to constitute the whole is a principle spice, although many unique differences may surface from time to time. The true spirit of covenant so commingles us that these perceived differences have no ability to divide us. This means that every person must be committed to maintaining the heart of the Father during trying seasons.

The Father's heart allows us to see things with clarity and understanding, not selfishly. It also creates the protocol to speak into one another's lives without muddled motives. Our motives, at times, have the ability to mute us to one another. Generally, when these times arise they are for covenant partners to recognize their own strengths and weaknesses and for them to live and portray God's merciful love. It is also a wonderful opportunity for us to apply and exercise all that we have learned. God gives us wide parameters of grace and we must do the same for each other. Covenant gives us a context in which to suffer long and allow the Lord to press us together for His glory, as grapes pressed to make new wine.

NETWORK GROWTH

One of the most difficult challenges and dangers every network eventually faces is expansion. This is the idea of extending exoterically to become greater in size and scope. Inevitably, expansion happens because of network friendships and the conquering action of a Kingdom mentality. Friends begin to share with friends about the mutual blessing and benefit of networking. Rosalie Mills Appleby captures the reality of friendship with this thought: "Friendship is the greatest opportunity to demonstrate our capacity for lofty and ennobling relationships without the motive of selfishness."[11]

In admonishing the Philippian Church, Paul stated:

> *If you've gotten anything at all out of following Christ, if his love has made any difference in your life, if being in a community of the Spirit means anything to you, if you have a heart, if you care—then do me a favor: Agree with each other, love each other, be deep-spirited friends.*   Philippians 2:1-2 TM

If we keep selfishness out of the equation, unexpected complications will not appear in network expansion. Selfishness has the ability to run amuck. The frenzy of it counters network growth and releases contraction as a counterbalance.

Jesus and the twelve disciples are beautiful examples of this point—He called His network partners *friends*! They had developed such a freedom in being together that it was cemented in friendship. Life is filled with many blessings, and we each need family and friends with whom to share these blessings. Thomas Hughes said:

> Blessed are they who have the gift of making friends, for it is one of God's best gifts. It involves many things, but above all, the power of going out of one's self, and appreciating whatever is noble and loving in another.[12]

Those in network relationships must guard against the possibility of repeating religious history's cycle. Network growth is the natural evolution of a *move of God*, an authentic flow of God's Spirit. The real peril of growth is in reproducing a network denomination. When this happens it necessitates a hierarchy of leadership, not necessarily emphasizing the empowerment philosophy. Such paradigms have led to aggressive forms of competition and denominational politics. In some cases, men begin to scheme, connive, and maneuver to ascend the leadership ladder. At this point, the network must diagnose the seriousness of the problem or begin the primary stages of recycling. Only servant-leaders will detect this phenomenon and make the necessary adjustments.

On the other hand, it is impractical and ridiculous to think that vast numbers of local churches and extra-local ministries could all be in intimate relationships with one another. Jesus demonstrated the circle of twelve. Though He had many thronging Him, He related intimately with twelve men. The philosophy of empowerment allows every network to develop various levels of relating. Each network carries a family DNA, thus keeping the family identity consistent. This is neither sectarian, sequestering, or seclusive; it's the principle of family. However, unique expressivity allows different network family members to flavor the network with cultural distinctions and different measures of the grace of God.

Network leaders understand that the driving force within the network operating system is not cloning. It is a sincere desire to deploy the present reality of the *finished work* in all the Earth! This is the message of truth with which the Church must come to grips. Experience tells us no two people will ever communicate that truth exactly the same way. The character and content of the message may be the same; however, brethren will minister their distinct portions based upon their God-given ministry abilities.

Networks must remember that God is not in the business of manufacturing skilled marketing agents selling the network franchise. Also, networks should never be about ministers forming the newest fellowship club, where once or twice a year pilgrimages are made just to renew credentials. Networks are about covenant, plain and simple. Anything else is a violation of God's heart and may be tainted with impure motives. Someone may ask, "What about network tasks?" All network tasks should be the direct byproduct of covenantal relationships, just as children are the byproduct of marital intimacy.

Leaders must discern, we are not producing the next mega-movement in Church history through the network concept. Once something becomes a *movement*, shortly thereafter it stops *moving*. New movements often attract disgruntled ministers and offended people from the previous thing God was doing. Many of them tried to invalidate God's dealings in their lives. I have found this never works on any level of relationship—period. Although every network vision should have universal appeal and worldwide ramifications, it is extremely important to be prudent in this matter. Bear in mind networks are about the union of intimacy between partners. Building with impoverished lives without this understanding can lead to some very difficult problems within the network operating system.

Herein lies wisdom: Network fellowship is about intimacy, transparency, and integrity. Sociologists have proven men and women always feel closer to those in relational proximity to them. An anonymous quote says it best:

> They who have loved together have been drawn close; they who have struggled together are forever linked; but they who have suffered together have known the most sacred bond of all.[13]

When network partners understand this, it deters jealousies, insecurities, and all types of network glitches. In fact, it is difficult to build intimately when insecurities are hidden within the foundation of the building. Global networks are to colonize the world with the Gospel of the Kingdom, which demolishes every other kingdom. Strong, satisfied, stable, and secure partners are the greatest resource to accomplish this feat. Suffering is the sacred bond that enables us to trust the integrity of one another's intentions as we each seek to participate in such an honorable vision.

WHEN AND WHERE DO WE START?

There is no better time than *now* to begin global reformation through networking wineskins. The Holy Spirit alerts the Church by saying it is time to wake up! Listen to His voice as it vibrates across generations of Church history, commanding the Church to *put on Christ*.

But make sure that you don't get so absorbed and exhausted in taking care of all your day-by-day obligations that you lose track of the time and doze off, oblivious to God. The night is about over, dawn is about to break. Be up and awake to what God is doing! God is putting the finishing touches on the salvation work he began when we first believed. We can't afford to waste a minute, must not squander these precious daylight hours in frivolity and indulgence, in sleeping around and dissipation, in bickering and grabbing everything in sight. Get out of bed and get dressed! Don't loiter and linger, waiting until the very last minute. Dress yourselves in Christ, and be up and about!

Romans 13:11-14 TM

The first Reformation occurred during the Renaissance Period. Renaissance means rebirth. Much pain and bloodshed laid the groundwork of opportunity. Servants of God could not waste time or squander the *kairos* moment—they had to be spiritually assertive. In secular fields, it marked a great reawakening of interest in literature, arts, and philosophy of ancient Greece and Rome. It birthed a questioning and critical spirit, a spirit of skepticism. Men forsook their devotion to institutions and yielded to strong individualism. The Renaissance man finally matured in the twentieth century to exemplify consummate selfishness.

THE RENAISSANCE NEW MAN

We are facing a new kind of renaissance today—it is a cosmic renaissance! It is not based in the skepticism of past failures in the first Adam, but in the optimism of the *finished work* of the last Adam, Jesus Christ. Our future is much brighter than we could ever believe. Jeremiah said the Father had a *future and hope* for us. (See Jeremiah 29:11.) The Church is like a root coming up out of dry ground after two millennia of lifeless, disjointed dogmas. Like Israel's favored son, Joseph, God is with His Church, expressing

approval as we hunger for Him. The favor of the Father pre-
fixed our destiny before we ever arrived in the twenty-first
century. Our union life with Him is one of association, companionship, completion, and process. We have exchanged
all that we were for all that He is! Union begins with Christ
being revealed to us—we die. When Christ is revealed in us—
we are replaced. (See Galatians 2:20; Second Corinthians
5:14-15.)

Very simply, favor finds its greatest reality in the Old
Testament concept *Immanuel*, which means "God with us."
(See Isaiah 7:14.) In the New Testament, it is *syn Christo*,
which is "together with Christ." (See First Thessalonians
5:10.) The Holy Spirit used this concept 12 times, a governmental number, to show the completeness of the work of
Christ. From death in Him to sharing His rule, we have an
immense future. Note these examples as they flow from
death to fullness of life. Christ is enthroned more and more
and Adam is dethroned and destroyed for the beast he is.

- We were crucified with Christ. (See Romans 6:6;
  Galatians 2:20.)
- We were buried with Christ. (See Romans 6:4.)
- We were united with Christ when He was planted
  in burial. (See Romans 6:5.)
- We were raised up together with Christ. (See Eph-
  esians 2:6; Colossians 2:12.)
- We live with Christ since we died with Him. (See
  Romans 6:8; Second Timothy 2:11.)
- We are made alive together with Christ. (See
  Colossians 2:13.)
- We are glorified together with Christ because we
  suffer with Him in sonship development. (See
  Romans 8:17.)
- We are made joint heirs with Christ. (See Romans
  8:17.)
- We are being changed into the similarity of form
  with Christ. (See Romans 8:29.)

- In full resurrection we will have conferred upon us the same form as Christ. (See Philippians 3:10.)
- Our glorious future necessitates endurance; therefore the Church reigns with Christ. (See Second Timothy 2:12; Revelation 5:10.)

The time to start is now! We must not squander these precious daylight hours as the Lord shines brightly in us. God has delivered us from the "point of origination" of our problem: Adam! The old, carnal family tree is cut down. (See Matthew 3:10.) Most of our current problems cannot be blamed on old Adam anymore. They are a result of our own *ruts*—our open-ended graves created by spinning our wheels in self-centeredness and self-righteousness. Our fiery trials have allowed us to be misrepresented and deliberately misinterpreted. We have been brushed aside and passed over. For some precious men and women of God, your labor of love for years has been brought to ruins by the ambitions of men with no scruples. To you, I say, "Fret not!"

Like Joseph of old, you are being prepared for something much greater than present circumstances. Affliction was his cross. It was the instrument used to cut him off from the old source of natural life, which was Jacob and Canaan. For us it is the attitudes accompanying denominational or non-denominational wineskins, flavored by everything except unity. The school of the Holy Spirit taught Joseph how to network in order to preserve nations during a time of famine. He was a Kingdom impact man who came into the full favor of the Lord.

The model of Joseph's life speaks to us of the things we must release to the Lord and forget about holding others guilty. Our sense of fairness is usually clouded by undeveloped character anyway. We must forgive everyone whom God has used as an instrument to accomplish His purposes in our lives. (See Genesis 50:15-18.) It is God's business whether He vindicates us or not. By being marked of God, men and women of God will be falsely accused without an opportunity for justice. I have found it is far better, and it takes a broken person, to abolish the desire for retaliation as Joseph did. (See Genesis 50:19-20.)

No doubt about it, somewhere along the line others have taken unfair advantage of you. It probably wounded you deeply. Nevertheless, stop bleeding all over the place— it's time to heal! Heal and comfort those who wounded you just as Joseph and Jesus did. (See Genesis 50:21 and John 20:24-27.) When we realize God was in all of our development and chastening, it enables us to express the creative uniqueness of our potential in Christ without reservation and fear. God meant everything we have gone through for our good.

The Tabernacle of Moses is our visible parable to teach us the proper ethos of reformation. It took all the priests and Levites networking together to maintain a proper sacrificial system. There are many valid networks today attempting to show God's people the proper approach to God: *It is through unity.*

The operations of the Feasts of Passover and Pentecost were essentially temporary arrangements until this hour of a complete overhaul of all things. Internally, we are being cleansed by the glory of God in our consciences. As Saint Augustine said, "A good conscience is the palace of Christ; the temple of the Holy Ghost; the paradise of delight, the standing Sabbath of the saints."[14]

The Church is finally coming to maturity. The time is *now!*

ENDNOTES

1. James Strong, "Greek Dictionary of the New Testament," *The New Strong's Complete Dictionary of Bible Words* (Nashville: Thomas Nelson Publishers, 1996), #1357, #3717.

2. *Webster's New World College Dictionary, Third Edition,* Victoria Neufeldt, ed. (New York: Simon & Schuster, Inc., 1997), 1128.

3. Geoffrey W. Bromiley, *Theological Dictionary of the New Testament, Abridged in One Volume* (Grand Rapids, MI: William B. Eerdmans Publishing Company, 1985), 1108-1109.

4. Adapted from William Smith, *Smith Bible Dictionary* (Grand Rapids, MI: Zondervan Publishing House, 1948), 657-58.

5. Bromiley, 1112-1113.

6. Strong, "Greek Dictionary of the New Testament," #652.

7. Virginia Ely, *I Quote* (New York: George W. Stewart, Publishers, Inc., 1947), 187.

8. *Webster's*, 282.

9. James Strong, "Greek Dictionary of the New Testament," *The New Strong's Exhaustive Concordance of the Bible* (Nashville: Thomas Nelson Publishers, 1984), # 4801, # 4862, # 2201.

10. *Webster's*, 984.

11. Ely, 141.

12. Ibid., 140.

13. Ibid., 141.

14. Ibid., 94.

Chapter Three

BEARING THE TORCH OF REFORMATION

This new plan I'm making with Israel
  isn't going to be written on paper,
  isn't going to be chiseled in stone;
This time I'm writing out the plan in them,
  carving it on the lining of their hearts.
I'll be their God;
  they'll be my people.
They won't go to school to learn about me,
  or buy a book called God in Five Easy Lessons.
They'll all get to know me firsthand,
  the little and the big, the small and the great.
They'll get to know me by being kindly forgiven,
  with the slate of their sins forever wiped clean.
                              Hebrews 8:10-13 TM

Schools of ministry, prophetic centers of the Holy Spirit, and apostolic training centers all had one goal at the close of the twentieth century: to prepare a generation to carry the torch of the Kingdom into the new millennium at a higher level. Everyone knew that current Church operations were subnormal to first-century Kingdom manifestation, and they needed reforming. This is not to imply the Church needs to return to a first century mentality—that's defeating God's purpose behind Kingdom advancement. Although we are more comfortable looking back than looking ahead, vision for the future is most important. If God's highest ideal was in the embryo of the first century, His Church would have stayed there. However, the postmodern Church must have first-century power to demonstrate the Kingdom. God is flexible enough to allow each century to have its own unique wineskin model.

Without contradiction we knew the Lord was beckoning our generation. We had all the signs of spiritual weakness, psychological weariness, and revolutionary predispositions. The last 50 years produced a generation who had forsaken the beautiful Gothic cathedrals and their padded pews for a more meaningful relationship with Christ and other believers. Some believers became so disenchanted with every form of controlled Christian gathering, they resorted to Christian services via television or e-mail. Baby boomers (those born from the end of World War II until about 1964) were all beyond the biblical age of maturity, which is 30. They should have been ready to supply communities with leadership, but were much like the generation that followed Joshua and his contemporaries.

> *Now Joshua the son of Nun, the servant of the Lord, died when he was one hundred and ten years old.*
>
> *And they buried him within the border of his inheritance at Timnath Heres, in the mountains of Ephraim, on the north side of Mount Gaash.*
>
> *When all that generation had been gathered to their fathers, another generation arose after them who did not know the Lord nor the work which He had done for Israel.* Judges 2:8-10

It is obvious baby boomers did not have the collective reputations of the World War II generation. That generation of men and women were called the greatest generation in American history. These champions of patriotism along with their allies defeated the diabolical insurgencies of fascist regimes in Germany, Italy, and Japan, bringing stability back to the nations of the Earth.

Because men possess little foresight for the future they assign the term greatest mainly to their past. To be the generation that follows those tabbed as the greatest is almost an impossible act to follow. Where do you go nationally except downhill from being the greatest? In Israel's history these great men and women of the mid-twentieth century compare to Joseph, the great statesman; Moses, the great servant; Eleazer, the great saint; and Joshua, the great soldier. Each of these patrons provided Israel with strong patriarchal leadership in very delicate, defining times.

The current Church age is demanding men of this magnitude in the Spirit to rise again. When Joshua's generation died, their children did not know the Lord or His works. They had very minimal knowledge of Egypt's defeat and the defeat of the two kings of the Amorites, Sihon and Og. (See Joshua 1:10.) That generation was so uninformed that they probably knew little of God's military genius as He executed victory after victory through Joshua and their fathers.

The men of Joshua's generation were so task-oriented, they forgot to train their sons in the art of relationship. This was very costly and deadly! The sons of Israel entered a cycle of backsliding that negated their ability to drive the enemies of the Lord out of their inheritance. I see the same problem today. Many of the Pentecostal fathers were busy defending their right to be acknowledged because of fierce persecution from their contemporaries. They either forgot or delayed training their sons in the ministry, preparing them to succeed them. Because of this, the Church is weak and sickly. She has been cultured to live with sin, sickness, poverty, and death. It is high time these four horns go to their designated place of judgment. Since sin, sickness, and poverty are by-products of death, they receive the same sentence as death: The realm of death is cast into the lake of fire. (See Revelation 20:14.)

REFORMATION: ANSWER TO MORAL DECLINE?

Moral decline will only be resolved through reformation—not revivals and renewals. There must arise a generation like Hezekiah, the reformer, who established godly priorities, both in character and deeds. He came from an extremely dysfunctional situation. His father, Ahaz, had left Judah in a very perilous and dreadful condition.

> *For the Lord brought Judah low because of Ahaz*
> *king of Israel, for he had encouraged moral decline in*
> *Judah and had been continually unfaithful to the Lord.*
> 2 Chronicles 28:19

This is a concise summary of a leader who committed wicked acts and engaged in some of the most heinous atrocities of Israel's history. When Judah was brought low, they came into a place of national humiliation. The Hebrew word translated as low is *kana*, which means "to bend the knee; hence to humiliate, vanquish: bring down (low), into subjection, under, humble (self), subdue."[1] The emphasis is upon a proud, independent, and recalcitrant spirit becoming abased. When this is the condition of leadership, people suffer by becoming naked and exposed. They are uncovered. (See Second Chronicles 28:19.) The common ingredient seems to be moral decline; therefore, no vision. (See Proverbs 29:18.) We must remember that where there is no vision (fresh, prophetic revelation of God), the people are undisciplined or get out of hand. In fact, The Modern Language Bible: The New Berkeley Version in Modern English says, "People run wild!"

There are several examples in the Scriptures where men are morally debased, and yet others are experiencing the fresh presence of the Lord in renewal and reformation. These men bear the torch of reformation. God never seems to leave Himself without a positive witness, no matter what the circumstances are. Note these examples: Noah, Moses, Joshua, Samuel, and Jeremiah.

Noah is the ninth son in the lineage of Adam as it descends from Seth. His prophetic assignment was to bring comfort as his father, Lamech, discerned the purpose of God for him. God would start a brand-new order through Noah and cleanse the Earth that had the accursed ground.

Mankind was never personally cursed! The ground was cursed for his sake. (See Genesis 3:18.)

> *Then the Lord saw that the wickedness of man was great in the Earth, and that every intent of the thoughts of his heart was only evil continually.*
>
> *And the Lord was sorry that He had made man on the Earth, and He was grieved in His heart.*
>
> *So the Lord said, "I will destroy man whom I have created from the face of the Earth, both man and beast, creeping thing and birds of the air, for I am sorry that I have made them."*
>
> *But Noah found grace in the eyes of the Lord.*
> Genesis 6:5-8

Hundreds of thousands of people had probably lived on the Earth by Noah's day. Certainly this was not the first case of a serious problem meriting judgment. Something very defining had begun to happen! The sons of God (godly seed) began to mix with the daughters of men (fleshly seed), thus supplementing a hybrid in God's purposes. A process had already begun to recover mankind from sin's tyranny. God's plan to recover man through the seed of the woman (see Genesis 3:15) was now in jeopardy. The same woeful excuse is the reason for man's faltering judgment—physical attractiveness succumbing into lustful behavior. When the sons of God entered into union with the daughters of men, they produced a giant, a bullying tyrant that opposed God's purposes in every age. Abraham, the children of Israel, David, and many others had to deal with that bullying spirit as it matured from age to age. Today, it is called the spirit of the antichrist. Christians have been so focused on looking for a person that they have missed the principle. This spirit has always been set to oppose the true Christ (Head and Body) from coming in the flesh. The heavenly Father, however, had a plan in Noah's day.

Noah finds grace, a fresh sense and understanding of God's omnipotence, while others are totally corrupted in the seedbed of creativity, which is *imagination*. Some people miss the mark through ignorance, while others are very intentional. There were special sacrificial offerings for sins of ignorance; however, willful disobedience carried profound consequences. These verses reveal the severity of moral decline in Noah's generation. God had no other choice but to judge this situation and begin anew with Noah as the new federal head of the race. Noah and his sons were blessed and given the opportunity to start God's purposes afresh with a new emphasis. The same command Adam carried generations earlier finds its residence in Noah.

Moses is another major fathering figure in Israel's history. The proof of his fatherhood is Joshua, the son of Nun. Moses was constantly dealing with the children of Israel's rebellion and challenges to his authority. Often they would vex his righteous soul, leaving him vulnerable to anger and intemperance. The following scenario is one of those occasions.

> *Now when Moses saw that the people were unrestrained (for Aaron had not restrained them, to their shame among their enemies),*
>
> *then Moses stood in the entrance of the camp, and said, "Whoever is on the Lord's side—come to me!" And all the sons of Levi gathered themselves together to him.*
>
> *And he said to them, "Thus says the Lord God of Israel: 'Let every man put his sword on his side, and go in and out from entrance to entrance throughout the camp, and let every man kill his brother, every man his companion, and every man his neighbor.'"*
>
> Exodus 32:25-27

Moses and Joshua had just come from the mountain in the presence of the Lord. God had sustained them for 40 days on His presence, giving Moses moral absolutes for the nation to function covenantally. While they were having an encounter with the Lord, the people were down below having their encounter with flesh. Joshua, still in leadership training, did not discern the true condition of the people at first. This is not highly unusual because discernment is not a chief virtue of youthfulness. Notwithstanding, under that covenant judgment was swiftly executed and the righteousness of God vindicated. Once again, we can see the principle of some finding grace while others were disgraced.

When one identifies with "being on the Lord's side," there may come circumstances in which we must affirm that decision. Many times we will have to stand for principle, sacrificing personal feelings. If we are led by our emotions in vital decisions, it may have the ability to cloud our reasoning. Immature Christians usually flow more out of emotions than wisdom. God is longing to raise a priesthood that will follow His commands to the letter. That may take sacrifice and a commitment to kill what must die in order to go on to the next level in God. I have discovered the Lord will not make that decision for us. He'll provide the grace to make the decision, but He'll never trample upon our right to decide. Normally we see death as permanent and terminal rather than transitional. Rarely do we see the seed of the next thing God is doing in the dying off of the previous thing He once did.

The third example of the Old Covenant nation showing a need for major reformation is during the judgeship of Eli. God uses Eli to mentor Samuel, who becomes a transitional vessel between Israel's judges and kings. Samuel's ministry parallels John the Baptist's in this sense: Both were used of God to present the next major fathering figure in the Kingdom economy. Samuel presented David and John introduced Jesus.

> *Now the sons of Eli were corrupt; they did not know the Lord.*
>
> *Therefore the sin of the young men was very great before the Lord, for men abhorred the offering of the Lord.* 1 Samuel 2:12,17

The priestly sons of Eli were extortionists and highly toxic. They were covetous, despicable, and they disrespected the established principles of God's law. While this priest-hood is negligent and deteriorating, God is developing Samuel, who becomes an impeccable model of character and priestly dignity. Samuel receives a prophetic word of judgment for the current system that confirms what God had spoken through a no-name prophet. (See First Samuel 2:27.)

Once again we can see the seed of the new order protected and carefully guided by God the Father into Kingdom order. Eli was a *destructive daddy* whose fatherly instincts had gone awry. He failed to correct his sons, thus crippling them. This is a classic case of fatherlessness, although the daddy is within the same proximity as the children. Unfortunately, by growing up in this environment, Samuel followed this malignant example. His sons did not walk in his ways, triggering a premature desire in the people of Israel for a king. (See First Samuel 8:3-5.)

First, this proves that even great men may fail to discern a problem and may need the assistance of others. Secondly, it may not be proper to judge a man or woman of God on the basis of their children's behavior. After being taught the things of God correctly, our children are still individuals who must make quality decisions of their own.

During the prophetic period, as the voices of the Major Prophets—Isaiah, Jeremiah, Ezekiel, and Daniel were heard, Israel was in another of her many low, disgraced places. Jeremiah, known as the *weeping prophet*, described the decline of social conditions. Note how his heart ached for men to be truthful with one another.

> *"And like their bow they have bent their tongues for lies.*
> *They are not valiant for the truth on the Earth.*
> *For they proceed from evil to evil, and they do not know Me," says the Lord.*

"Everyone take heed to his neighbor, and do not trust any brother; for every brother will utterly supplant, and every neighbor will walk with slanderers.

Everyone will deceive his neighbor, and will not speak the truth; they have taught their tongue to speak lies; they weary themselves to commit iniquity."

Jeremiah 9:3-6

I would never place myself on par with Jeremiah; however, my heart frequently aches because of the lack of integrity in the Church. Jeremiah was passionate. He pleaded earnestly a heartbreaking message to a stiff-necked and obstinate people. Reformation is essential when the standard of truth has become nil in society. A qualifying mark of moral deterioration is an inability to trust. It is equally true today! Most homes are locked, dead-bolted, and have bars on the windows because people cannot trust each other. Many church buildings have been pillaged and raped of equipment just to satisfy someone's addiction.

This is a vast, negative change from my boyhood days in North Carolina. Neighbors respected and watched for one another. We felt so secure that most nights we did not lock the doors. Things have certainly changed for the worse! When I visited South Africa, I found certain cities as much or more decadent than America. The ugliness of apartheid left them with severe moral breakdown and distrust. Some men even place electric wires at the top of fences that surround their properties. The lack of social and moral health in communities is an unfailing index of moral decline.

This same moral decline has reached into the pulpit and pews of the postmodern Church. Preachers now contract before preaching the Gospel; certainly proving it is more beneficial to have a corporate business mentality rather than a spirit of brokenness. Covenants are broken before the words, "I'm committed to you," are out of the mouths of people. Marriages are in shambles. Long-term commitments to congregations by pastors are a foregone conclusion, yet most people make career moves without considering the call of God.

The Church has become an axis of dishonesty—a paradox to the spiritual intent of the original words Jesus uttered: "I will build My Church" (Mt. 16:18). Some men no longer allow the Lord to direct their steps in itinerant ministry—they are led by mammon. Nothing short of reformation will change these glaring discrepancies.

REFORMATION ACCESSIBILITY

When we go back to the Scriptures and note the sovereignty of God at work in Hezekiah's life, it's fairly simple to see why he initiated one of Israel's greatest reformations. If we could profile this wonderful 25-year-old man, it would look something like this:

- Hezekiah was raised in a dysfunctional family in which there was much liberty and very little godly restraint. His father, Ahaz, probably did not provide any moral absolutes.
- Hezekiah's primary male models were all wicked examples of selfishness, lawlessness, disorder, and absence of divine government. Ethically, there was strong deterioration.
- Economically, the nation was in shambles. Moral decline usually guarantees economic disaster—either recession or depression.
- Hezekiah's mother, Abijah, whose name means "worshiper of Jehovah," was obviously a chief influence in his life. Her disposition for worship shaped his perspective concerning the worship of Jehovah.
- At the age of 25 Hezekiah was probably just developing his personal niche, discovering what his kingly orientation would be, and starting to come away from some of the young adult frivolity.

- Hezekiah had his mother's sensitivity, which came from her father, Zechariah, whose name means "Jehovah has remembered," and who had understanding in the visions of God. *Remember* is a word of covenantal consciousness. In Hezekiah's spiritual root system there was a consciousness of covenant and worship.

The Bible says that Hezekiah "did what was right in the sight of the Lord, according to all that his father David had done" (2 Chron. 29:2). He reopened the doors of the house of the Lord, which was an act of reformation. Prioritizing correctly, he did it in the first year and the first month of his reign. A man's purpose can be calculated by what he deems as urgent priorities. Reformation is impossible if God doesn't have an open door of entrance and utterance into the lives of His people.

There were several crucial decisions Hezekiah had to make in order to turn the nation around. Speaking of a heavy burden! This was quite a load on the shoulders of a 25-year-old man. As the chief influencer in the nation, whatever decision he made would affect everyone. It all began with a positive action—opening the doors to the *house of the Lord*—implying he had opened himself to the Lord. Several questions would be answered as God found a place among the people once again. From the pristine days of Genesis until the current times, God has always sought residence among mankind. He is such a gentle God—He never forces the issue, always recommending our need to open to Him.

What is involved in "opening the doors" to the house of the Lord? Every door requires a key that is specifically designed for that door. The spiritual key for Hezekiah and for us is to "set our affections to do that which is right in the sight of the Lord!" (See Second Kings 16:2.) Biblical affections are mind-sets and thought patterns, implying moral interest and reflection. Reformation releases an intimacy with the Lord that is derived out of spending time with the

Lord, reflecting upon Him and His interests. There can be no deep, lasting reformation without the relentless pursuit of the Lord, even if it means experiencing the crushing blow of the cross along the way.

What is the "expectation" of opened doors in the house of the Lord? It is realistic to expect a *prophetic visitation* that slams the door to a system that has no open vision. God introduces an *apostolic and prophetic priesthood* that has been conditioned in the crucible of divine delay. As the Lord receives an open door into the hearts of His priesthood, they receive an *open Heaven* into God's heart. The opened Heaven is maintained by an effectual, *opened prayer life* (see Lk. 11:10), which leads to *opened eyes* (see Lk. 24:31) and an *opened book of revelation* (see Lk. 4:17; Rev. 5:1-10). In Exodus 19, God opened the Heavens, descended onto the mountain as His own voice, and He opened the *book* of His own purpose. In this current reformation, the continued open Heaven gives a continual view of the Ark (Christ Jesus). Lay Jesus over the Tabernacle of Moses and the Tabernacle's furniture will line up with the pierced points on His body during His passion. He is the *only view* that matters in the Heavens. (See Revelation 11:19.) Everything about the Tabernacle of Moses must speak first and foremost of Jesus Christ. Jesus is the highest representation of the presence of God. The Revelation is a revelation of Jesus and all things in relationship to Him. The Feast of Tabernacles unveils the Ark (Christ Jesus), the contents of the opened book.

What is the release of *open doors* in the house of the Lord? First of all, there is an *open fountain* of cleansing to God's people. (See Zechariah 13:1.) The fountain is made available in Passover; it is *applied* in Tabernacles. This same fountain washes away sins in Passover, and it removes the stain and purges the conscience in Tabernacles. Open doors give an unobstructed view into a realm of new perspective essential for the removal of self-will. (See Isaiah 52:1-2.) If we use the five senses of our humanity as a guide, the eyes would be the apostolic, which is for direction or seeing. Sight sustains us—we recognize the moment as an *open opportunity* to fully identify the who, the what, the when, and the where of God's doings in the Earth. (See Jeremiah 40:4.) Finally, there is an *open praise* of full deliverance before the Lord, who has unwrapped the graveclothes of death and thrown them off of us. (See Psalm 102:16-22.) The first priority to prepare a generation to carry the torch of reformation is *openness*. In God, it is impossible to change or shift into greater Christlikeness if one remains closed.

REFORMATION AND SANCTIFICATION

The second major objective on Hezekiah's agenda was to gather the priests together and command them to sanctify themselves and the house of the Lord God. (See Second Chronicles 29:4-5.) The term *sanctify* occurs frequently in the Old Testament Scriptures. This Hebrew word from which sanctify is translated is also rendered as dedicate, consecrate, sanctuary, hallow, and holy, but especially by the word *holy*, and often *holy one*. It appears some 700 times in its various forms. One of the names of Jehovah is Jehovah *Mekaddishkem*, which means "the Lord who sanctifies you."[2] (See Exodus 31:13; Leviticus 20:8; 21:8; 22:32; Ezekiel 20:12.)

Sanctification is the process by which *saints* are made. Saintly believers become the tools of reformation. *The Expanded Vine's* says, "Sanctification is thus the state predetermined by God for believers, into which in grace He calls them, and in which they begin their Christian course and so pursue it."[3] Anyone who has sought sanctification has found it impossible to achieve in human strength. It is a relationship entered into with God that men experience by faith in Christ. (See First Corinthians 6:11.) The Spirit of God is the agent of sanctification. (See Romans 15:16; Second Thessalonians 2:13; First Peter 1:2.) He separates us unto the Lord and Christ sanctifies and cleanses us with the laver of His Word. (See Ephesians 5:25-26; John 17:17.) Christ presents us as holy, blameless, and above reproach in His sight. (See Colossians 1:22.) Sanctification is the will of God, and it keeps the believer out of illicit affairs without covenant (See First Thessalonians 4:3-4.) God did not call us unto uncleanness, but unto holiness and sanctification.

Sanctification is man offering to God, under the unction of the Holy Spirit and grace's awning, total dedication to His purposes without any human resistance. There were a number of special events in the Scriptures that demanded sanctification. This short list provides examples of how insistent God was about sanctification before transforming moments that shaped Israel's history.

- The giving and receiving of the *Law* (See Exodus 19:10,14, 22-23.)
- The ordination of the *priesthood* (See Leviticus 8:30.)
- The raising of the *tabernacle* as a *sanctuary* (See Numbers 7:1.)
- *Israel* in preparation to cross the *Jordan River* (See Joshua 3:5.)
- The prophet Samuel anointing *David* as *king* (See First Samuel 16:5.)
- The *Levites* and *priests* in bringing up the *Ark of the Covenant* (See First Chronicles 15:12,14.)
- The *priests* in bringing the *Ark* into the *Temple* (See Second Chronicles 5:11.)
- The *priesthood* and the *Temple* during the *reforms of Hezekiah* (See Second Chronicles 29:5,15,34.)

In the days of King Ahaz, Judah became an adulterous, idolatrous society of outcasts intoxicated on heathenism. Foolishly they followed the pursuits of the heathen nations. They sacrificed their sons in the fires of Molech just as postmodern America is sacrificing her sons to the butchers of abortion. The enemies of the Lord were honored and respected when they should have been confounded and crushed. Young Hezekiah had to follow this detestable decadence with a regenerated idea of God. It was time to expose a system that rendered the Lord of glory to a place of disrepute before the nations.

Sanctification is more than separation, which is the most basic way people have interpreted this word. It is more than a position or relationship in regard to the Lord; it is also participation in the nature of the Lord, His character and His works. The process of sanctification brings man to a place to accept God's unblemished uprightness as well as His radiant, majestic holiness. Sanctification compels men to eagerly pursue God in the midst of an evil and adulterous generation. It is the antidote for the secularization of mankind initiated by humanistic philosophies of life from unregenerate, antagonistic thinking. Sanctification is the overt response to a world that has turned away from the one true God.

By experience, most believers acknowledge sanctification is definitely a moment-by-moment work. It is a progression leading to much deliverance. Whatever has caused man to separate from God, his fellowman, himself, and nature is healed essentially in sanctification. The Holy Scriptures speak of creation (nature and the universe) awaiting fulfillment through mankind coming into personal fulfillment. That's the reason it works hand-in-hand with reformation. Because of the perfecting excellence of continual reformation there is a realization of utter and absolute surrender to the Lord. Surrender and sanctification often clap their hands together. God's unique work by the Holy Spirit and man's participation in sovereignty merge to give a proper view of sanctification.

In Matthew 5 the New Testament unveils six foundations of sanctification in relationships:

1. Sanctification from *anger* leading to *murder* (See Matthew 5:21-26.)
2. Sanctification from *lust* leading to *adultery* (See Matthew 5:27-30.)

3. Sanctification from *divorce* leading to *covenant-breaking* (See Matthew 5:31-32.)
4. Sanctification from *frivolous oaths* and *unholy speech* (See Matthew 5:33-37.)
5. Sanctification concerning the *spirit of retaliation* (See Matthew 5:38-42.)
6. Sanctification unto God in *perfect love* (See Matthew 5:43-48).

Reforms under Hezekiah produced a work of sanctification that became the internal touchstone of reformation. Hezekiah summoned the Levites and commanded them to sanctify themselves and everything connected with the Temple worship. The Levites removed the filthiness in the holy place. (See Second Chronicles 29:4-5,16-19.) Much uncleanness was present as Judah forsook the Lord and became involved in paganism, which paralleled the condition in Jeremiah's day. Israel chose a system that produced no renewal, revival, or reformation.

> *For My people have committed two evils: They have forsaken Me, the fountain of living waters, and hewn themselves cisterns—broken cisterns that can hold no water.*   Jeremiah 2:13

God's children have such a propensity to trade the divine for the human, which is actually frightening. The seed of this began in Adam, who reached for carnal knowledge and closed the Heavens. This created a carnal, humanistic condition in mankind. Initially, mankind was introduced in a high state as the image-bearer of God. Anything hewed (human) has definite disadvantages or limitations, whereas the fountain of living waters is infinite. Whatever we hew will always break! It has the stroke of death in it because it is the invention of human device and challenges divine restraint. All sectarian denominations have become *hewn cisterns*. I could have just as easily said *human* cisterns. Distinctions are not evil in themselves; in fact, God gets great joy out of diversity. But when they are saturated with a spirit of denominationalism, distinctions coupled with pride become an evil God refuses to bear.

Another interesting work of sanctification was the destruction of *the serpent of brass*. (See Second Kings 18:4.) For almost 800 years Israel made a mountain out of a molehill. Finally Hezekiah, armed with the spirit of reformation, had the courage to deal with this tragic symbol of a former move of God birthed out of Israel's rebellion. (See Numbers 21:9.) This serpent had become an icon of idolatry. Alarmingly, most of the first generation Israelites died in the wilderness, but the serpent made it out! Now, it is considered part of the filthiness kept in the Holy Place.

This is very important to catch! The Holy Place in the Tabernacle of Moses parallels the Pentecostal economy of the Church. I am persuaded that the greatest filth in the Church is our unholy theology we have concocted about the devil. Although some habits and addictions may be destructive forces, they pale in comparison to the fetish the Church has about the devil. As with the Levites in Hezekiah's day, it is time for the priesthood of believers in the New Covenant to crush the serpentine spirit under their feet. We must not be hoodwinked any longer! The time has come to divest ourselves of Pentecostal folly and Charismatic chaos, which almost presents the devil as being on equal footing with God. The adversary is not God's rival as such. This diabolical spirit is a subject, just like everything else in the universe.

Judah confused the reality of what and whom to worship. Their need to worship was tarnished with idolatry. Through the medium of sanctification, their worship was realigned with the principles of God and they longer suffered at the hands of misinformation. Hezekiah had instituted reforms that produced an unparalleled move of God in the Old Testament. The priests transported the uncleanness of the Holy Place into the Brook Kidron. *Kidron* means "dusky place,"[4] and *dusky* means "lacking light; dim; shadowy...gloomy; melancholy."[5] The implication of this word is

117

mourning, sackcloth or sordid garments, and a state of repentance and transition. Reformation demands that people change their minds and move with the cloud of God's new doings.

Two great kings also crossed this brook at defining moments in their lives and kingdoms: David and Jesus. David crossed during his flight from Jerusalem during Absalom's rebellion. (See Second Samuel 15:23.) The Scripture reveals that this was a time of deep repentance, brokenness, and consternation. He refused to allow the priests, Zadok and Abiathar, to bring the Ark of the Covenant with them during this time of God's dealings. David strictly placed his future, if he had one, into the hands of Jehovah, who had given him the kingdom. He was personally purged during these times and received his own crushing blow of the cross on the Mount of Olives.

Jesus crossed this brook on His way to Gethsemane. (See John 18:1; Mark 14:26; Luke 22:39-46.) *Gethsemane* means "oil press." The anointing without measure was in *Christ*, which means "anointed one." Gethsemane was the ordained place in which the individual Christ would be crushed as an olive berry and prepared to fill the *corporate* Christ on the Day of Pentecost. As Jesus prayed and agonized, He began to release His life (blood) in drops of sweat as they profusely rolled off His body. The intensity of the moment and the weightiness of creation on His shoulders fractured capillaries. As a representative man, Jesus' decision was mankind's decision. This was the opportunity to rectify what Adam had wronged. Adam chose to practice his rights to decide for himself; whereas, Jesus totally relinquished His will to the Father.

The mark of distinction in both situations—David's and Jesus'—was betrayal by someone in their inner circle. David had Ahithophel and Jesus had Judas. (See Psalm 41:9; 55:12-14; Second Samuel 15:12;16:23; John 13:18.) They were both key personnel and of great importance to kingdom affairs. Each man could have become a "who's who" in the kingdom if he had resisted treachery's claws. In each case, it became a time of purging and cleansing—a kingdom transition in which death takes place! David would be a different king when he returned to the throne. Jesus died and came forth in another form. He lives before the heavenly Father, but He also lives in His corporate Body. So, the Brook Kidron has a history of being associated with monumental kingdom changes.

After the priests and Levites cleansed the Temple, thus cleansing the Kingdom, it was prepared for the next wave of Kingdom glory and activity. Judgment always begins at the house of the Lord. (See First Peter 4:17.) Amazingly, all the rubbish was removed within eight days, which speaks of a new beginning. What King Ahaz had made unclean through years of irresponsibility was now clean. The Scriptures particularly mentioned the altar of burnt offerings with all its articles and the table of shewbread with all its articles. (See Second Chronicles 29:18.) The burnt offering and the shewbread both speak of Christ and His *finished work*. Burnt offerings in the Old Testament spoke of Christ totally being set ablaze by Jehovah's fire. When His body is broken in crucifixion and remembered in resurrection, it is the truth of the shewbread. The shewbread also speaks of the communion table—the broken bread of His body, and the cup of communion.

The byproduct of a cleansed people, a cleansed sanctuary, and a cleansed priesthood is a new heartfelt attitude of worship. The object of all reformation is to bring people into a renewed place of worship after the due order of God. Worship is both *motion* and *emotion*! These are the channels to release the depths of love and adoration that generate in the heart of men as they are drawn into the presence of a loving heavenly Father. Worship is the opposite of man-centered and self-centered love, which is recognized by two manifestations: manipulation and greed. The hearts of Israel were released to give as they worshiped. There was such abundance that the priests and Levites returned to sacred tasks and left the fields of secularism. God's divine order was rightly restored. And whenever God's order is man's order, abundance is the result.

REFORMATION AND INTIMACY

In John 14 Jesus spoke to His disciples about reconnecting with the Father. He mentioned the Father more than 20 times in this chapter. Jesus used the phrase "in the Father" several times, highlighting the principle of intimacy. The high point in John 14 is verse 23: "Jesus answered and said to him, 'If anyone loves Me, he will keep My word; and my Father will love him, and We will come to him and make Our home with him.'"

Love is the motivating factor of all intimate relationships. God loves us unconditionally; therefore He chooses to make His home in us. It is so dishonoring to the context to use this chapter to substantiate doctrines Jesus never taught. He would go to the Father to reestablish our legal right to reconnect. The only thing John 14 teaches is that Jesus is *the way* to intimacy with the Father. We all can be mansions, or *dwelling places*, of intimacy. A mansion from Jesus replaces our old, decrepit, shanty tent from Adam. Many mansions are in no other arena than where the Body of Christ is! A mansion of continuous fellowship and intimacy is what we are to the Father. I long to see the day when the Church can establish a sense of solidarity about this point. Our worship will drastically change, and much of our theological folly will cease.

Worship addresses the need for intimacy between the Creator and His creatures. Mankind was created for God's pleasure, created to worship Him in spirit and in truth. Thanksgiving and praise may be corporately expressed; however, worship is very personal and uniquely experienced. Revelation chapters 2–3 address the Church that had lost her sense of intimacy because of an adopted religious culture rather than one of worship. These chapters reveal there is *corruption* in the *Church*, *trash* in the *treasure chest*, and a *mess* within the *message*. As in the example of the first Adam in Genesis 3, the Church had lost the place of complete intimacy with the Lord—that place of being naked without the cloak of serpentine subtlety. In the Revelation of Jesus Christ, the opening address to the representative Church of Ephesus is a clarion call back to intimacy. (See Revelation 2:1-7.)

One of the keys to ministry is intimacy with the Almighty. The early apostles spent every hour of more than three years with the Lord. Can you imagine the impact of abiding in His presence this way? From my earliest days of being aware of the calling of God, this became a priority and emphasis in my life too. I can remember the many times the Lord required me to come away with Him into the high places of separation. My heart certainly had the ability to become fragmented and cluttered, and I was in great need of divine refreshment. Sometimes I was so impressed with the sense of accomplishing things *for* the King, I failed to remember the King. Over and over I have had to ask myself, "Are you leaving ample room for the Lord in all of your endeavors?" It can be a great risk to our personal reputations and a terrible disappointment to expectant believers when we choose to leave working for Jesus to become intimate with Him.

God's requirements may be stringent at times, but I have found that they are always for our good. While learning the basics of the Bible, the Lord required me to stop watching television for a while. This continued for a period of almost two years. As much as I love competitive sports, I could not tell anyone who won the Super Bowl, NCAA Championships, the World Series, or anything else. My assignment was to be intimate with the Almighty. During this time of quiet meditation, the Lord spoon-fed me the Word of God and began preparing me for my current assignment. I came to realize quickly how the Father trains and prepares Kingdom servants. It all starts with a *holy hush*! As in the case of Moses, the Lord may invite you away with

THE SOUND THAT CHANGED EVERYTHING

Him and not show up for days. In the process, while waiting on Him, we learn to desist—our demands turn into total abandonment unto the Lord.

As a young boy in the Baptist Church, I remember our pastor opening every service with this statement: "But the Lord is in His holy temple. Let all the Earth keep silence before Him" (Hab. 2:20). Not having the slightest idea what this Scripture meant, the congregation responded to the call to worship and thus sang the opening hymn. After many years of studying the Minor Prophets, the Father has clarified my lack of youthful imperceptiveness. I have come to realize that this Scripture, along with several others, is a call to intimacy with the Almighty. It's a divine time-out, a call to cease from our labors and attitudinally come into His presence with holy reverence.

Through the years, I have discovered David's attitude is what the Father expects to retrieve from us in intimacy. Listen to these poignant words of the sweet psalmist:

> *Lord, my heart is not haughty, nor my eyes lofty. Neither do I concern myself with great matters, nor with things too profound for me.*
>
> *Surely I have calmed and quieted my soul, like a weaned child with his mother; Like a weaned child is my soul within me.* Psalm 131:1-2

David had simplified his life without becoming a simpleton. He did not focus on continuous issues of life. He chose to quiet himself. Intimacy with the Lord weans us from all the distractions in life that could cause a detour from Him. From these verses it is clear that there is an element of spiritual maturity that is childlike. We are not too busy or too deep to take time for *Daddy!* Other Scriptures that capture this same truth are the following:

> *Be silent in the presence of the Lord God; for the day of the Lord is at hand, for the Lord has prepared a sacrifice; He has invited His guests.* Zephaniah 1:7

> *Be silent, all flesh, before the Lord, for He is*
> *aroused from His holy habitation!*   Zechariah 2:13

Not fully realizing it, the Church's mundane activities are her angst; she craves intimacy with the Lord. One more new twist on the same program is not going to cut it. Preaching with a sixteenth-century mind-set in a twenty-first century time slot won't either. Using *Webster's* definition *intimate*,[6] we could say that intimacy is marked by close association, acquaintance, or familiarity; relating to or characteristic of one's deepest nature; that which is essential, fundamental, very personal, and marked by privacy and informality.

The Lord has bidden us to come into a vital and quality relationship with Him. This is personal and requires the removal of all masks because God does not regard anyone's mask. We are His invited guests! Our problem is: *We're too busy!* In every instance in which the Lord began a new approach in extending the Kingdom of God in the Earth, He required intimacy with His subjects. Moses had to get away in the Old Covenant; the apostles had to retreat in the beginning of the economy of Pentecost; and now we, a new vanguard, must come away to the mountains of separation and hear the Father's heart for the implementation of the Feast of Tabernacles.

The final address to the Church in Revelation 3 is to the Church of the Laodiceans. It is an invitation to return to intimacy. (See Revelation 3:15-20.) If we allow each church to represent a specific epoch in Church history, the Laodiceans would represent most of modern Christianity. She was an affluent church with much stuff, but not necessarily the right stuff. She had many carnal evidences of the blessings of the Lord. However, she is continually naked! This does not imply the nakedness of intimacy. It is the temporary state of being uncovered that indicates a church lacks intimacy.

The Lord stands at the door of our hearts and He knocks. If we open to Him, it will be just as the Scripture ingenuously intimates:

> *My beloved put His hand by the latch of the door,*
> *and my heart yearned for Him.*
> *I arose to open for my beloved, and my hands*
> *dripped with myrrh, my fingers with liquid myrrh, on*
> *the handles of the lock.* Song 5:4-5

If we clutch the Lord's hand in intimacy, it will cost us. We will enter into the fellowship of His sufferings and unequivocally enter the power of His resurrection. *Myrrh* means "bitter"![7] The resin was collected by distilling drops taken from canals in the inner bark of the tree. It naturally secreted through cracks, fissures, or wounds, or from incisions intentionally made in the bark. It had a pleasing fragrance, yet a lasting, bitter, aromatic taste. *Smith's Bible Dictionary* says myrrh was used for embalming, anointing, medicinal purposes, and purification.[8] In the collection of myrrh, the task is underwritten with the principle of the Cross. Wounds! Cracks! Fissures! Each of these terms suggests brokenness, which perfumes the fellowship of intimacy with the Lord. The purity of suffering with the King through the command of His Word produces a free, liberated, and spontaneous flow of His life.

The call to intimacy becomes the bookends of God's call to the universal Church in Revelation chapters 2–3. Pregnant with living hope, we are standing in such a strategic time in the history of mankind. As an Ephesus church, we may have arduous labor without unfeigned love. Smyrna reveals that one may be aggressively persecuted by the ungodly without persevering through their taunts. Pergamos is a church of great spiritual insight without impeccable integrity. Thyatira is a church of tremendous spirit but seduced under a spirit of sexual immorality. Sardis is a church of outstanding programs without positioning the posterity for growth. We all know the perils of the Laodicean age—great acquisitions without inner, spiritual substance to balance them. If there is one redeeming factor in the messages to the churches, it is in the message to the

Church of Philadelphia. Believers can love God, love one another, and prove that intimacy works!

If we open the door to the Lord in this new dispensation, He will come in by virtue of His desire for intimacy. The Church has become so conditioned to "five easy steps to everything: prayer, prosperity, studying the Scripture, etc..." Intimacy is beyond the reach of "easy steps, and just like that, you're there." Like John in Revelation 4, there is a command to "come up," or arise into another realm in God. That realm is saturated with a new intimacy. We may choose to stay in the earthly plain of Revelation 2–3 and simply speak of beasts, harlot systems, false prophets, Church problems, and Charismatic chaos. This will not change anything.

The real action is in Revelation 4. Our steps are reordered and Church confusion seems less overbearing in that realm. This chapter signifies a new order of reformation for the Earth. It pictures a sovereign God speaking like a trumpet from a new perspective. The throne, and not the earthly theater of human failure, becomes the center of attraction. There is One on the throne in appearance like jasper and sardius stones. These were stones in the Old Testament High Priest's breastplate. (See Exodus 28:15-21.) According to the command of God, they were set in order of the birth of the sons of Israel. Reuben, the firstborn, was assigned the sardius stone; and Benjamin, the twelfth son, was given the jasper. Each name pictures an aspect of our sonship experience. Reuben is sonship potential and possibility! Benjamin is sonship maturity and total development! The reversal of order in the Revelation speaks of a people apprehending the purpose of God completely. The first shall be last, and the last shall be first. Our experience shall overtake our potential, and thus God's desire to have a many-membered son conformed into the image of Jesus Christ will be fulfilled.

This new reformation is a global opportunity for all nations. However, we must come higher if we are to reach God's ideal. The first reformation started in the European nations and reached into the New World as men separated because of religious persecution. The second reformation was conceived primarily in North America and has moved into other nations through the American gospel enterprise. Although much has been accomplished, we have peddled some wares that are unconscionable.

It is my belief that much of the third wave of reformation will be found in developing countries of what we call Third World nations. The vast majority of the Earth's population centers can be found in these nations, and we know God does not remain in any one setting all the time. I believe it is in order to issue a warning to North American Christians: *If we do not move with God, we will soon be first-world in technology but third-world in Kingdom experience and reality.* God is moving on! Our theologies have boxed us in and made us look foolish. A prime example of this was the Y2K debacle at the close of the twentieth century. The Church, in North America particularly, appeared to have no discernment. A new breed of money launderers made a killing from our ignorance and failure to discern the times and seasons of God. Only when we risk coming higher will our view change. If we will come higher, our datelines and linear concepts will be swallowed up into a greater reality of the finished word and work.

If I use the Tabernacle of Moses as my chief revelatory principle of the Scriptures, three significant concepts depict the nations in connection with the throne: before, around, and in the midst of the throne. The Ark of the Covenant within the Holy of Holies is God's throne. *Around* the Tabernacle are all the tribes, representing the nations in their assigned order. *Before* the throne is a prophetic/priestly company, laboring together with the Lord in the work of the ministry. However, *in the midst of the throne* are the overcomers, who have been granted to sit with the Lord in His throne. The overcomers will come from all the tribes of the Earth. This is not some sectarian concept disallowing certain people groups. The price is one and the same for all nations:

overcoming! Through intimacy with the Lord, we each have an equal opportunity to reach the place of overcoming.

The torch of reformation will be carried by an international agency that has willingly stood before the Lord on a "sea of glass" (Rev. 15:2). Whether one sees this as the laver in Moses' tabernacle or the sea in the Temple of Solomon, the principle is the same. The torch of reformation will be borne by a Kingdom embassy of people who have met the requirements of sanctification. The only difference in this group versus other groups who have charted the course of reformation is in the word *crystal*. When speaking of the people of God, this is a beautiful thought! *Crystal* speaks of anything congealed and transparent, a kind of precious stone. The Father will have a people as clear and as transparent as Jesus was. There will be nothing between Him and them! No one in the Old Covenant ever became totally transparent! Bearing the torch of the Kingdom reformation will be on such standard bearers in this new millennium. Revelation 4 closes with this new embassy recognizing the difference between their *creation* and their *vocation*. We are created to worship the Father. All reformations lead to worship—period. The Altar of Incense, which is the altar of prayer and praise, is positioned right in the heart of the Tabernacle. The Tabernacle is symbolic of Jesus. His heart is a heart of worship.

ENDNOTES

1. James Strong, "Hebrew and Chaldee Dictionary," *The New Strong's Complete Dictionary of Bible Words* (Nashville: Thomas Nelson Publishers, 1996), #3665.

2. The Bullinger Publications Trust, "Appendix 4—The Divine Names and Titles," *The Companion Bible* (Grand Rapids, MI: Zondervan Bible Publishers, 1974), 6.

3. John R. Kohlenberger III, ed., *The Expanded Vine's* (Minneapolis, MN: Bethany House Publishers, 1984), 555.

4. Strong, "Hebrew and Chaldee Dictionary," #6939.

5. *Webster's New World College Dictionary, Third Edition,* Victoria Neufeldt, ed. (New York: Simon & Schuster, Inc., 1997), 422.

6. *Webster's*, 707.

7. Strong, "Hebrew and Chaldee Dictionary," #4753.

8. William Smith, *Smith's Bible Dictionary* (Grand Rapids, MI: Zondervan Publishing House, 1948), 426-27.

Chapter Four

HARNESSED FOR CHANGE

Come to Me, all you who labor and are heavy laden, and I will give you rest.

Take My yoke upon you and learn from Me, for I am gentle and lowly in heart, and you will find rest for your souls.

For My yoke is easy and My burden is light.

Matthew 11:28-30

Can two walk together, unless they are agreed?

Amos 3:3

These who have turned the world upside down have come here too.   Acts 17:6b

These people are out to destroy the world, and now they've shown up on our doorstep, attacking everything we hold dear!   Acts 17:6b TM

The late Bill Britton, one of the fathers and statesmen of the modern Feast of Tabernacles message and a powerful prophetic scribe, wrote an excellent tract, "The Harness of the Lord." The Holy Spirit gave him a compelling vision that spoke of the Lord's discipline and the people's response. The vision chronicled the development of two young colts, one rebellious and the other submissive. They had the opportunity to observe the unshakable reliance of mature horses that had submitted to discipline and had learned to obey the master's voice perfectly. I offer this summary of that tract.

Both colts were in the open field, foot-loose and fancy-free. The only thing they knew about life was free play, without restrictions or responsibilities. Privileged to have the lariat noose placed around their necks, they were led off to the master's corral for training and discipline. Each colt was sad their freedom was taken away. They became restricted in a confined environment surrounded by a fence. There was no place to escape! The trainer began to work with them with the whip and bridle, and what a death this was, since they were not free to do as they pleased anymore. Both colts initially interpreted this experience to be more horrible than anything they had encountered in life.

One colt rebelled and the other submitted to the harness. The rebellious one found a way to jump the fence and head back to the grass meadows, the free range. The other colt decided to submit his will and learn the ways of the master. If there had never been training or testing, there would never have been submission or rebellion from either of the colts. For in the field, they were innocent without rebellion or submission.

The training finally ended for the submissive colt. He was rewarded with greater confinement. The harness was dropped about his shoulders and his freedom was to move only when he heard the master's voice.

While nibbling on the grass in the field, the rebellious colt saw the King's carriage being drawn by six horses. With amazement, he saw his brother as one of the lead horses on the right side. His brother was now made strong from the corn in the master's stable. Thus he complained: "Why has my brother been so honored, and I am neglected?" He awakened to the startling reality that the master had not chosen him for the wonderful responsibility of pulling his carriage.

Famine came into the land. The rebellious colt ran in circles seeking green pastures. The brother was fairing well in the master's stable. Finally, he asked his brother, "How do you remain so healthy in a time of famine?" An answer came from a voice of victory and praise: "In my master's house, there is a secret place in the confining limitations of his stables where he feeds me by his own hand, and his granaries never run empty, and his well never runs dry."[1]

The interpretation of this vision is too obvious to miss. God's harness leads to greater freedom and confinement at the same time. What some people call legalistic is actually the only route to true freedom in the Lord. Although entering the harness is a process, it lends to a people developing spiritually. The essence of spiritual maturity may be understood in this verse from the Scriptures, "And He who sent Me is with Me. The Father has not left Me alone, for I always do those things that please Him" (Jn. 8:29).

When people are harnessed, they must always do the things that please the Father. *The Message* paraphrases John 8:29, "The One who sent me stays with me. He doesn't abandon me. He sees how much joy I take in pleasing him." As we are harnessed for change, our delight is in pleasing the Lord perfectly.

YOKED TO BE HARNESSED

Jesus invited weary travelers, who were being proselytized by aggressive Jewish evangelists, to come unto Him and receive His rest along with His yoke. This was actually one of several messianic war cries. To all today who are weary from the numbing effects of the Babylonian, religious system, the same clarion call roars from the lips of the Master, "Come to Me!" Most Christians have come unto everyone and everything *but* Him.

I have found it may be an easy yoke and a light burden; however, it is still a *yoke*! Historically yokes were wooden frames consisting of a crossbar with two U-shaped pieces that encircled the necks of draft animals. The *neck*, which is symbolic of the will of man, was the direct object of yoking. The first thing the Lord does when we come to Him is slip His yoke on our wills. Many believers think yokes are demanding, demeaning, and confining. Perhaps most think they should distance themselves from any type of yoke. The prophet Jeremiah certainly did not agree with that kind of thinking. He said, "It is good for a man to bear the yoke in his youth" (Lam. 3:27). The yoke captures us and prepares us for the harness because harnessing goes beyond the initial phase of yoking.

Webster defines the harness as "the gear or tackle, other than the yoke, of a draft animal."[2] A draft animal is one that participates in a *team venture* for the purpose of pulling or drawing a load. This is a metaphor to describe disciples and those broken and disciplined by the hands of our loving High Priest as He develops us into a team. Harnessing produces a close association with the thing we are harnessed for. Since God has harnessed us to be conformed into the image of Jesus Christ, that requires change after change. Now we must learn how to harness the change. To reject the Lord's harness is to reject change and to constantly remain in a state of immaturity.

HARNESSED BY COVENANT

The Church will harness change as she accepts this truth across the board: God has committed Himself to building a covenantal family as an emerging force of integrity and destiny in the Earth. *God will get what He wants!* In the Heavens, we are members of a *seamless whole* rather than the discordant fragments we appear to be on Earth. Destiny speaks to our appointment, whereas integrity speaks to wholeness. The appointment of the twenty-first century Church is to partake of the Feasts of Tabernacles. It commences with the blowing of the trumpets on the first day of the seventh month, which is actually *a sound that changes everything*!

Divine appointments relate little to uniformity of belief about theological preferences and nonessentials. God's appointments compel us to form a multiplicity of expression, thus manifesting the true diversity of unity. It is very pertinent for all individual ministries and local churches to discern with whom God has purposed them. The timing of the appointment and the recognition of the *appointed place* will become apparent after that.

In both the Old and New Testaments, the Heavens flowed by fixed, ordained appointments in the Earth. Actually, nothing was done outside of prearranged appointments. The Earth is the *seen form* of the unseen realities of the Heavens that functions by the principle of "the fullness of times." There can never be a haphazard barging into the things of God without first receiving an invitation. The Hebrew word that sets this principle in our thinking is moed, which means "an appointment, i.e., a fixed *time* or season; spec. a *festival*;...by implication, an *assembly* (as convened for a definite purpose); technically the *congregation*; by extension, the *place of meeting*."[3] *Moed* speaks to how definite God is about doing things by appointment:

- There is an *appointed time* for which a godly vision is intended and enforced. (See Habakkuk 2:3.)
- There is an *appointed people*, who become the embodiment of any vision. (Old Testament = the nation of Israel; see Exodus 19:3-6. New Testament = the new nation, the Church; see First Peter 2:9.)
- There are *appointed festivals* and *solemnities* for the appointed people. (See Leviticus 23:2; Deuteronomy 31:10-13.) Appointed festivals are *holy convocations* in which there were rehearsals of all God had done. Rehearsal may be divided into these parts: *re+hears+all*! For us today, it is a rehearing of all God has accomplished in Christ. This is the reason convocations are so vital to the life of the Church.
- There is an *appointed place* for the appointed people to gather. In the Old Testament it was earthly Zion. (See Psalm 132:13-18.) In the New Testament it is spiritual Zion, New Jerusalem. (See Hebrews 12:22-24; Revelation 3:12; 21:2,10.)

Every feast has an appointed time to be fulfilled in the earth. The first two feasts, Passover and Pentecost, have been fulfilled with those appointed of God to experience them. Now, it is time to move on! The prophet Amos' question comes to mind here: "Can two walk together, unless they are agreed?" (Amos 3:3) Very practically, "Can the Church continue to walk with God without coming into agreement with Him?" The answer is emphatically *no*! We cannot agree with God unless we know *what* He is doing, *how* He is doing it, and *where* and *when* He wants to do it.

Sadly, we have thought God wanted to build mansions in the Heavens, as though the Heavens were incomplete. In fact, He wanted to build *us* as a mansion in the Earth all the time. God is searching for a human being, a generation to agree with Him. The real issue of covenant is: God desires to bring us into a supportive companionship with Himself in this Earth, and thus His purpose is finished through mankind's co-participation. I am concerned that the time is running out for this current generation to catch this truth. Our assignment is to be harnessed together with God, becoming His apostolic messengers and burden-bearers in the Earth. There are no burdens to bear in Heaven.

WORLD CHANGERS

The Church has the assignment of being *world changers*! Collectively we must have God's *worldview* in order to accomplish this. A *worldview* is "a comprehensive, esp. personal, philosophy or conception of the world and of human life."[4] In his book, *Understanding the Times*, David Noebel defines *worldview* as "any ideology, philosophy, theology, movement, or religion that provides an overarching approach to understanding God, the world, and man's relations to God and the world."[5] The Church has been so Heaven-bound, we have not adopted a mandatory, comprehensive worldview that mirrors the heart of God for the Earth. Anything comprehensive is broad in scope, showing extensive understanding.

As we progressively move into the mind of Christ, our worldview will evolve and change many times because no one phase of our development has a lock and key on all God is doing in the Earth. Thirty years ago Christians primarily believed our worldview should be preparation to evacuate this planet by the year 2000. Of course, this changed as we realized that we had canned theologies with too many eschatological superstitions based upon carnal interpretations of the prophetic writings.

Please note that inherent in change is movement. Change always involves going from one place or position to another. Change implies that the current state of affairs is in need of some type of transposition. For example, in music transposition means "to rewrite or play (a musical composition) in a different key or at another pitch level."[6] Change often comes in order to alter the original expression because for some reason the total effectiveness is in question. When it comes to certain aspects of our theology, great alterations are needed. Theologically we are still living in the sixteenth century when it is now the twenty-first century. Many are operating from a Gutenberg printing press mentality in the midst of a global superhighway paradigm. I would say change is in order.

Most of the mega corporations of the postmodern world understood this and adjusted their worldview in the last decade. Fundamentally, there was no way to remain competitive in a global market without corporate mergers and consolidations. For example, I mainly use Delta Airlines for most of my business travel. Delta has partnered in the air with Aero Mexico, Air France, Air Jamaica, China Southern, Czech Airlines, Korean Air, Malaysia Airlines, Singapore Airlines, South Africa Airways, and United Airlines. This gives Delta connecting routes into North and South America, Europe, Africa, Asia, and Australia.

Having nothing to do with fondness and a sense of brotherhood, these are strictly business connections and decisions. The company's brass saw an opportunity and had no delusion of grandeur about their individual strength. Delta was wise enough to also partner with more than thirty hotels and resorts and six car rental companies. In addition to this, Delta has agreements with MCI, Nextel, American Express, Visa, E*TRADE, GMAC Real Estate, Lending Tree, North American Mortgage Company, Radisson Seven Seas Cruises, Renaissance Cruises, and 1 (800) FLOWERS.COM. All of these are financial institutions that mutually benefit Delta Airlines.

You may be asking, "What's the meaning of all of this?" The answer is quite simple—if we will read the forecast clearly. Remember, change is necessary when the current state of affairs is inadequate. Jesus said, "For the sons of this world are more shrewd in their generation than the sons of light" (Lk. 16:8). The world understands the exponential power of combining resources and coming together. In an article from *The New York Times*, The Chase Manhattan Corporation, the third-largest banking company in the United States, negotiated to acquire J.P. Morgan & Co., one of the most prestigious banks in the world. Chase was striving to transform itself into a global financial powerhouse, and acquiring Morgan would sharply accelerate the process.[7] From this article, it was clear that Chase had to have a global economic worldview to remain competitive.

As the writer of the Book of Hebrews stated, when speaking of all the faith-worthies in Hebrews 11, we do not have the time or space to discuss medical consolidations, energy mergers, media mergers, computer technology mergers, and so on. The point is clear: The wave of the now and the future is mergers and consolidations. A more insightful question may be: "When will the Church realize networking is far more effective than existing on some tiny island, alone, in self-delusion?" We lean toward reinventing working wheels rather than supporting them. Networks must combine resources and work together for the good of the Kingdom of God. Worse yet, it's arrogance for any one network to think it can canvass the whole world.

TENETS OF CHANGE

Paul and his apostolic networking team models an apostolic thrust that became world changers. They had a reputation in the Roman Empire of destroying the old regime of religious secularism and were not endorsed. The angry mob of Thessalonica was one group voicing a negative opinion of them. They said, "These people are out to destroy the world, and now they've shown up on our doorstep, attacking everything we hold dear!" (Acts 17:9 TM)

In regards to the ministry of Paul in Thessalonica, it is worthwhile to read the epistle to the Thessalonian Church. Here Paul tells of his entrance into the city, after leaving his torturous experience in Philippi. (See First Thessalonians 2:1-20.) Many elements of harnessing change are supported in Paul's experiences in Thessalonica.

The first element of any change is to respectfully give honor to the last thing God was doing before the new administration started. God said to Joshua, "Moses My servant is dead" (Josh. 1:2). The Father spoke highly of Moses by eulogizing him as His servant. He did not degrade or disrespect him in any manner, although Moses had made a grave error. It didn't change God's mind! Moses was still His appointed man. Divine Providence always has a specific reason in selecting men and women of purpose to fulfill certain tasks. Paul acknowledged the Jews as the previous move-of-God people in his day.

> *For I am not ashamed of the gospel of Christ, for it is the power of God to salvation for everyone who believes, for the **Jew first** and also for the Greek.*
>
> Romans 1:16

The last major moves of God in our day have been the Charismatic Renewal, the Prophetic Renewal, and the River Movement. Smaller revivals have come out of these three. The heavenly Father used each movement to awaken the Church to spiritual realities, thus enabling her to vacate carnal information that had weakened her foundation. No movement was purposed to usher in the coming of the Lord Jesus, although that was the predominant thinking of the time. So, no movement could mature the Church by itself and prepare a spotless bride. It would take something more profound, with a greater proficiency, to convince the Church that her real goal is to be conformed into the image of Jesus Christ.

Apostolically we must reason from the Scriptures as Paul did. Lasting change cannot be executed upon the subjectivity of human desire and emotions; but there must be a recognizable, prompt objectivity of God's Word that this is God's ordination. *Reason* is the Greek word *dialegizomai*, meaning "to reckon thoroughly,...to deliberate (by reflection or discussion)."[8] Apostles must be clear about the whole counsel of God (see Acts 20:25-27), which consists of three feasts, not two. Thorough reasoning in the new millennium is to reason about the Feasts of Passover, Pentecost, *and* Tabernacles.

For apostolic ministry to be most effective in the twenty-first century, more forums of discussion must be established. This creates the opportunity for an exchange of views and not a monopoly of one viewpoint through media exploitation. Preaching is wonderful and I thoroughly enjoy it! However, it creates a society of pew-warmers more than serious seekers of the Lord. In this atmosphere, 20 percent of the congregation becomes involved while 80 percent vegetates in self-will on an emotional roller coaster. Unfortunately, a chasm exists between doers and hearers that is filled with vain imaginations, idols, and toxic opinions. People's growth becomes stunted when they are trapped in the web of extreme emotionalism and a gulf of idleness.

> Then Paul, as his custom was, went in to them, and for three Sabbaths reasoned with them from the Scriptures.   Acts 17:2

Using the method of reasoning, Paul established the Thessalonian Church in 21 days. That's quite a remarkable achievement! Most ministries require many years to establish them in the faith. A probable reason is the lack of apostolic and prophetic input in modern churches. For many years conventional scholarship incorrectly taught that apostles and prophets ended with the first-century church. My argument with this faulty reasoning is: How can you fully build and establish the Church without two of her most important tools of empowerment? Because of apostolic authority, Paul was able to enter the old wineskin—the synagogue—and prove Jesus was the Messiah. He had a knack for explaining and demonstrating; he had both the dogma and deeds of the apostolic function.

> *Explaining and demonstrating that the Christ*
> *had to suffer and rise again from the dead, and saying,*
> *"This Jesus whom I preach to you is the Christ."*
>
> Acts 17:3

Many immature believers have tried to change their old wineskins without delegated authority and have been met with stiff opposition and resistance. Adjusting or cracking wineskins is a delicate matter; and it is not a job for the ambitious, immature, or fearful. God has always placed this task into the able hands of apostolic ministers. They have a proven divine revelation, not a parroted-message, of the *finished work* of God, which is *Christ*.

Paul opens and alleges that Jesus of Nazareth is the Christ of God. He voices the truth and lays out scriptural evidence for proof. The Old Testament Scriptures are just sealed books until the Lord quickens them to us. Breakthrough revelation, by divine order, is usually given to apostles first. Apostles possess both the grace and the verve to deal with extreme opposition, which usually accompanies apostolic ministry. Jesus is the model apostle, who opened the covers of the Book of Himself. During His earthly ministry and after His passion, He continued to reveal Himself page by page.

> *Then He said to them, "These are the words which*
> *I spoke to you while I was still with you, that all things*

must be fulfilled which were written in the Law of
Moses and the Prophets and the Psalms concerning
Me."

And He opened their understanding, that they
might comprehend the Scriptures.

Then He said to them, "Thus it is written, and
thus it was necessary for the Christ to suffer and to rise
from the dead the third day."   Luke 24:44-46

In the final stages of preparation, Jesus continued to instruct the apostles, as Luke's account reveals. Incisive communication was imperative. There had to be an inspired belief in the revelation of Him as He is, and not the messianic illusions they had had prior to His coming. The same is true with every generation, as the message of reformation scintillates with revolution. Although we do not consciously seek to offend people, there are no grounds for neutrality in the midst of change. It is urgent that we catch what the Lord is saying to us! The Holy Spirit draws a line of demarcation, and we are either on one side or the other. Listen to Jesus again in one of His less than flattering moments.

I've come to start a fire on this earth—how I wish
it were blazing right now! I've come to change every-
thing, turn everything right side up—how I long for it to
be finished! Do you think I came to smooth things over
and make everything nice? Not so. I've come to disrupt
and confront! From now on, when you find five in a
house, it will be—
  Three against two,
  and two against three;
  Father against son,
  and son against father;
  Mother against daughter,
  and daughter against mother;
  Mother-in-law against bride,
  and bride against mother-in-law.
                          Luke 12:49-53 TM

Such powerful words: Jesus came to *disrupt* and *confront* everything. Our religious systems are so tidy and neatly placed, we fail to confront real issues today. Adam, the embodiment of carnality, the devil, the sin nature, and death were all confronted and tackled by Jesus. They would never again rise out of the dust of defeat. Unfortunately, the Jews did not understand His true motive was one of loving confrontation for the purpose of creating the right kind of Kingdom culture. They mainly took His words apart from the attitude in which He spoke them. This fostered a blazing offense in their hearts, which could not be quenched. Ultimately the nation of Israel and the Romans crucified Him.

The prophet Micah foresaw a day when men would have strong contentions against one another because of the fiery revelation of the Christ. (See Micah 7:6.) Most families who have had members leave the established familial wineskin and go to another experienced the *fire of estrangement* Jesus talked about. An enemy outside the family is one thing, but father or mother against son or daughter is too painful to ponder. It affirms the truth that civil wars are the most costly relationally and the bloodiest. Whenever Jesus taught, He would divide the multitudes with His teachings. (See John 7:40-44.) True apostolic teaching will have the same dividing affect today. Paul experienced this in Thessalonica.

> *And some of them were persuaded; and a great multitude of the devout Greeks, and not a few of the leading women, joined Paul and Silas.*   Acts 17:4

When the Kingdom of God is preached, make no mistake about it, people choose sides. One area of conflict is the teaching on money. A part of the Kingdom message is about finances. We must learn to deal with large sums of money in a world that has a Gross Domestic Product of over 40 trillion dollars. Unfortunately, we became very accustomed to dealing with poverty and lack in Pentecost. The Church must adjust and prepare to deal with prosperity and the people of prosperity, the aristocracy. Government officials and dignitaries will come into the Kingdom of God. Their wives may lead the way, as usual; nonetheless, they are coming! Although we have the poor with us always, we must create ministries to deal with people who are not poor. So much of gospel preaching has been to people with blind eyes, tin cups, and canes. I am not belittling this group because that's the group I came from. However, the Scriptures speak of the nations and the wealth of the nations coming into the Kingdom of God. Are we, the Church, prepared to deal with them? We must embrace an entirely different mentality and strategy in order to deal with *all people* God desires to incorporate into the Kingdom.

Spiritual leaders must find the nucleus that will join and align with them in the actual change and paradigm shift. All people will not make the necessary shifts to move with God. Some are satisfied with where they are spiritually and cannot see anything else. In Acts 16:13-15, Lydia wasn't such a person. She was a faithful disciple, and the Lord opened her heart to heed the things spoken by Paul. Because of the amount of concentration necessary when launching something new, we need everyone on the same page, hearing the same frequency. Paul said,

> *Now I plead with you, brethren, by the name of our Lord Jesus Christ, that you all speak the same thing, and that there be no divisions among you, but that you be perfectly joined together in the same mind and in the same judgment.* 1 Corinthians 1:10

New works thrive and can only be cultivated by those who are completely considerate of one another. Much labor is often wasted because apostles are dealing with people who are transfers from other situations and have not learned to share a common vision with any leader.

Paul was also very considerate of the women who labored with him. In Philippians 4:3, he said, "And I urge you also, true companion, help these women who labored with me in the gospel, with Clement also, and the rest of my fellow workers, whose names are in the Book of Life."

Why have women historically had a quick response to the Gospel? I believe women, as a whole, have less of an egotistical attachment to the traditions established by men, especially if they have had no part in developing them. The Gospel is a message that engages our emotions as well as our reason. Women are definitely more emotional, which doesn't make them less reasonable or unreasonable.

For 19 hundred years, the Church has developed some pretty deadly traditions of men that have caused many in succeeding generations to become caustic and bitter. Men's traditions, which have no biblical base, are like generational serial killers to the purposes of God. In fact, it is to the point that traditions have become brute beasts, antagonistic towards any progression of reformation in the Church. The new breed of apostles must not fear to be bold when battling these traditions. Remember, traditions make the commandment of God of no effect. (See Mark 7:13.)

Traditionalists use the rabble of human understanding to attack the new thing God is doing in the nations. (See Acts 17:5.) True spiritual warfare is not fighting the human agents opposing us in the Earth, but fighting the spiritual, unseen forces of darkness inciting traditions of men and vicious attacks to protect them. (See Ephesians 6:11-12.) Apostolic warfare is not according to the flesh. (See Second Corinthians 10:3.) Therefore, apostles cannot use carnal weaponry. Our greatest battle is always with human logic and reasoning. Devils already know they are subject to the name of Jesus and they fear Him. The culprit that must be convinced now is our logical, humanistic minds.

We must understand change in a Kingdom context: *Our world will be adjusted and turned upside down!* The way we conduct some of our Church affairs today will cease to be by the next decade. Change brings either a reformation or a riot in us. From the account in Acts 17, some of the women were reformed while some of the men rioted. Being acquainted with human nature, I am quite sure some men and women were indifferent to the Gospel's claims.

Because women have been spurned for many centuries, God will use them as leading spiritual forces in the new wave of reformation. Women will move with God while apologetic men will be arguing over the legitimacy of the move. How many ministries would all but fold if women left? The results would be startling if we would dare poll most churches in the West. It would probably be somewhere in the neighborhood of two-thirds. All this says is that while men are seeking positions of power and prominence, women are functioning and doing the work of the ministry.

Because we are harnessed for change, we must yield to King Jesus in a participatory manner. All the kings and gods of this age simply personify us ruling our own lives. The reason they are so plentiful is because humans never run out of creative ideas, establishing new gods as they go. Change attacks our idols and the existing political and religious establishment. We must not allow their intimidation tactics or bullying ploys to prohibit us from embracing God's changes. Because of change the landscape of the Church will gradually look very different during the twenty-first century.

Emerging in the twenty-first century will be a new apostolic Church that will be yoked and harnessed for change. At first, it must parallel the restoration of the judges in the Old Testament without their glaring weaknesses. (See Isaiah 1:24-26.) This Church will have two primary foci or centers of activity and attention: *possessing* the promise and *positioning* the posterity. (See Psalm 144:11-15.) Prophetically this Church will have a crystal-clear anointing of glory flowing out of Christ's life, without the impediments of natural talents and artificial anointings. What God is birthing is the *genuine article*. (See Revelation 22:1-5). There must be a sensitivity to the voice of God that brings one into a face-to-face encounter with Him, effectually adjusting all of society. Conforming to sub-Kingdom of God cultural expectations, politically-correct ideals, and the fear of man must be dashed against the Rock, Christ Jesus. This Church will practice biblical reconciliation between the races, the genders, and all classes of humankind. (See Galatians 3:26-29.)

I see a Church that understands the *spirit* of command, not the *law* of command. Like the beautiful chestnut horses in Bill Britton's vision, this Church will wait on the Master's voice. This Church will not be need-oriented, high-maintenance consumers. Since they are conformed into the image of Jesus, they will be Kingdom producers and people who finally understand their participation in the God-kind of life.

In the first Passover, which was actually a reformation period, Israel came out of Egypt under the hand of a shepherd/servant and lived from hand to mouth every day. They only knew God's acts and inherited nothing. (See Psalm 103:7.) In the Passover of Conquest, Israel inherited the promise under the hand of a soldier/servant, Joshua (see Josh. 11:23), who functioned by the spirit of command and required a "Sir, yes sir" mentality. These are the boundaries in the new order of command: Both banks will reflect a people who are *one with God*. And please remember, the spirit of command is never about some deluded, domineering, egotistical, self-absorbed maniac, who manipulates God's people for selfish motives or to feed some insecurity through the exercise of raw power.

As Paul and Silas traveled from Thessalonica to Berea (see Acts 17:10-15), they found eager, fair-minded people, who received the brethren and studied the Scriptures daily to see if what was spoken was true. In the twenty-first century, we must seek out those who are noble and fair-minded, willing to think creatively outside of the box. Modern man's stuffy theologies, carved out of archaic systems that have long ago served their purposes, must be adjusted. What we must decide is: Do we want relics or reality-based experiences?

Also, leave the philosophers alone. They are moved by the pursuit of wisdom and by intellectual investigation! Being lovers of thoughts, they are intelligent but not necessarily men of the Spirit. Because most of them are so confused in their own delusions concerning Christ, it makes no sense to argue with them. Christ cannot be reasoned out—He must be experienced. Philosophers see our King as an *unknown God*. Our God is beyond inquiries, penetrating analyses, and laws of cause and effect underlying explanations of His reality. To a philosophical mind-set, that kind of God is not worthy to be worshiped.

However, to us He is worthy to be worshiped and adored. This is the message the new apostolic Church must declare to the world. It is one of love, light, and life. It is captured in Paul's words as he preaches in Athens, Greece.

> *Therefore, the One whom you worship without knowing, Him I proclaim to you:*
>
> *God, who made the world and everything in it, since He is Lord of heaven and earth, does not dwell in temples made with hands.*
>
> *Nor is He worshiped with men's hands, as though He needed anything, since He gives to all life, breath, and all things.*
>
> *And He has made from one blood every nation of men to dwell on all the face of the earth, and has determined their reappointed times and the boundaries of their dwellings,*
>
> *so that they should seek the Lord, in the hope that they might grope for Him and find Him, though He is not far from each of us;*
>
> *for in Him we live and move and have our being, as also some of your own poets have said, "For we are also His offspring."*
>
> *Therefore, since we are the offspring of God, we ought not to think that the Divine Nature is like gold or silver or stone, something shaped by art and man's devising."* Acts 17:23b-29

I love the way *The Message*, with all its contemporary renderings, says it. If the New King James Version of the Bible doesn't speak clearly to you, this version will.

The God who made the world and everything in it, this Master of sky and land, doesn't live in custom-made shrines or need the human race to run errands for him, as if he couldn't take care of himself. He makes the creatures; the creatures don't make him. Starting from scratch, he made the entire human race and made the earth hospitable, with plenty of time and space for living so we could seek after God, and not just grope around in the dark but actually find him. He doesn't play hide-and-seek with us. He's not remote; he's near. We live and move in him, can't get away from him! One of your poets said it well: "We're the God-created." Well, if we are the God-created, it doesn't make a lot of sense to think we could hire a sculptor to chisel a god out of stone for us, does it? Acts 17:23-29 TM

The new apostolic Church is harnessed of God to make sure this message is proclaimed on every continent, in every tongue. When it is embraced, *it is a sound that changes everything!*

ENDNOTES

1. Bill Britton, *The Harness of the Lord* (Springfield, MO: The Church in Action, 1996).

2. *Webster II New College Dictionary* (Boston: Houghton Mifflin Company, 1995), 506.

3. James Strong, "Hebrew and Chaldee Dictionary," *The New Strong's Complete Dictionary of Bible Words* (Nashville: Thomas Nelson Publishers, 1996), #4150, #3259.

4. *Webster's*, 1540.

5. David A. Noebel, *Understanding the Times* (Eugene, OR: Harvest House Publishers, 1991), 8.

6. *Webster's*, 1422.

7. Patrick McGeehan and Andrew Ross Sorkin, "Chase Sets Sights on J.P. Morgan," *The New York Times*, September 13, 2000.

8. James Strong, "Greek Dictionary of the New Testament," *The New Strong's Complete Dictionary of Bible Words* (Nashville: Thomas Nelson Publishers, 1996), #1260.

Chapter Five

LET THE CHURCH BE THE CHURCH

And I also say to you that you are Peter, and on
this rock I will build My church, and the gates of Hades
shall not prevail against it. Matthew 16:18

The Church stands as a symbol of the finest aims and aspirations of the human heart. It has outlived persecution from
without and open disloyalty from within. It has withstood
bitter and unrelenting attacks of atheists and cynics of every
age. It has outlived changing times of peace and war, prosperity and depression, and many a fad and fancy.—Edgar A.
Guest.[1]

It was early spring and anxious believers, black and
white, of many different denominations, had gathered at
Deliverance Evangelistic Temple. DET, as most of the members affectionately called the church, was a progressive, clas-
sical Pentecostal/Charismatic church. Our roots were
Pentecostal and our operation Charismatic by 1975. There
had been no gathering in our fellowship or in eastern North
Carolina to compare with this event. Many men and women
of God were fully persuaded God was up to something big!

This was the second of three major transitional events in
our church during the decade of the 1970s. Dr. Derek Prince
and his ministry team were the expected guests. Dr. Prince was
part of a leadership team in Fort Lauderdale, Florida, commonly known in those days as the Florida Five. This group
consisted of Dr. Prince, Bob Mumford, Charles Simpson,
the late W.J. Ern Baxter, and the late Don Basham. Because
Dr. Prince was a well-known teacher and statesman in the

Charismatic movement, people had come with great anticipation from many counties within North Carolina. Through
Dr. Prince's writings and tape ministry, people became aware
of this historical and most important gathering.

At the time I was one of the young ministers growing
up in Deliverance Evangelistic Temple. Having been a
member of the church for four years, I remember the sense
of awe and gratitude I felt because God had highly favored
us. Other men of God had come in earlier years, but it paled
in comparison to this time. Like myself, most of the other
young ministers were enthralled. Not any of us knew exactly what to expect—we were just tremendously excited about
the looming possibilities.

The day of the first meeting finally arrived. Our expectation did not soar into disappointment. In fact, God
exceeded our highest anticipation and our most vivid imaginations. Some 1,100 people somehow crowded into a sanctuary that seated barely 750 people comfortably. Praise
songs such as, "He's the Lover of My Soul" and "The Glory
of the Lord," rang out with great enthusiasm. They became
the anchor songs of the meeting. Most people cared very little about the apparent lack of space. Only one thing mat-
tered: *God was in the house!*

God was prepared to teach us lessons on the Church,
His Body, and His family that would catapult us into a new
realm of anointing and glory. He was also ready to break the
grip of racism and denominationalism in eastern North Carolina. God released a sound in that meeting that changed
the lives of many people. Quietly, we each began to understand that, although our skin pigments and denominations
were different, we were indeed one body, born of the same
seed and bloodline.

Dr. Prince ministered powerfully and wonderfully in
British eloquence. He concentrated on the seven significant
pictures of the Church in the Book of Ephesians. The potential was there to mobilize into something great for the Kingdom of God. If the regional church polity, at the time, had

had an ear to hear what the Spirit was saying to the Church, there would have been a major divine explosion in the region. As usual, that same old tired question arose, "Who is going to spearhead what God is now doing?" Rather than allowing the Holy Spirit to lead, it seems men can't wait to take control of what God is doing. Oh, how often we forget! People are always looking for Saul, their king, when God lovingly desires to be King.

Paralyzing fears, partisan spirits, and former allegiances prevented men from embracing the *new day*. Many returned to their former cycles and have never been the same again. Very prominent individuals used their influence to work against the Lord's doings. A faint shadow of what the Lord could have accomplished was accomplished.

After considering that event almost 28 years later, I often wonder what the spiritual landscape in eastern North Carolina would have been had men discerned the Lord's timing properly. It is so unfortunate that there were very few men and women with the spirit of the sons of Issachar—men who had understanding of the times to know what Israel ought to do. (See First Chronicles 12:32.) Many believers have died since that strategic year, and others are still waiting for the *big bang* to hit again.

The big bang people are waiting for His Church to be thoroughly prepared in Kingdom manifestation—a many-membered, multiracial, and multicultural organism. The Church is His Body and the fullness of Him. It behooves each of us to understand what Jesus meant by the term "Church."

GREAT CONFESSION

Imagine being around, without question, the most amazing man you have ever seen. You are very puzzled as to why He asked you to follow Him, but day after day you obscurely follow! At first you did not perceive it clearly, but every other great man eventually pales in comparison to Him. He teaches and ministers with an authority the philosophers and Pharisees only dream of. Renowned for teaching by principle, parable, precept, and practice, He's bold to violate traditional Sabbath rules; He casts out demons and unclean spirits; He feeds the multitudes from the unthinkable; He walks on water; He heals the mute and the maimed; there's nothing impossible for Him! Even John the Baptist, an impeccable soldier of righteousness, cannot stand in His shoes.

Why has He drawn this motley crowd of dissidents unto Himself? Fishermen, zealots, farmers, and tax collectors all congregate together. Because they have no solid ground of relationship, their disdain for one another is very obvious in the Scriptures. It's now time to move them from the impressionable stage of wonder to the strategic stance of preparation. Their spiritual education must now move from courtship to commitment. What was once simple—just being with and watching Him—now becomes more complex. The setting is ripe for Jesus to be revealed as the Christ of God.

Things escalate in ancient Caesarea Philippi, which was built as a memorial to Tiberias Caesar and Herod Philip. Obviously, they are the two powerful secular leaders affecting Jewish life. According to historian Alfred Edersheim, Caesarea Philippi was picturesque, somewhat reminding one of locations in the Swiss Alps. He writes,

> Caesarea Philippi rose more than 1100 feet above the sea, and was very impressive and magnificent. The city nestled amid three valleys on a terrace in the angle of Mount Hermon. Everywhere there were trees, vines and vegetation, dashing torrents and fountains, reeds and rocks, and the mingled sounds of birds and waters. This is an extraordinary place of richness and beauty.[2]

In this setting, Jesus captures the moment to establish in their thinking the new thing God is doing in the Earth—His Church. It would be separated from every other *ekklesia* on the face of the Earth. Caesar had his, Herod probably had his, and no doubt other groups had theirs. Now, Jesus is about to birth His *ekklesia*.

It was in this chiefly Gentile region that Jesus and his small band retired after one of the many demands of the Pharisees to *show them a sign from Heaven.* (See Matthew. 16:1.) Also, it was here that His own probing question struck the hearts of His disciples and caused a response to spring from the lips of impetuous Simon Peter. In his true quick-triggered, sanguine nature, he said, "You are the Christ, the Son of the living God" (Mt. 16:16b). It is also conjectured that the rock wall below, the rock on which the castle stood, under which sprang the Jordan, supplied the proper metaphor for Christ's words, "You are Peter, and on this rock I will build My church, and the gates of Hades shall not prevail against it" (Mt. 16:18).

Now, the question eternity has recorded and rehearses for every generation under the sun is: "Who do men say that I, the Son of Man, am?" (Mt. 16:13b). Jesus knew the self-assured, conservative Pharisees and liberal, humanistic Sadducees were bitterly hostile toward Him. Because of institutionalized prejudice, one could not trust their assessment of Him. The masses were shallow and wanted only a political Messiah. They all had vague ideas about Him—no reality. Up to this time, the disciples were not much different. Frankly, they were not sure *who* He was! He couldn't be one of the prophets reincarnated because, although some members of the Pharisees taught it, most people did not agree with metempsychosis, the transmigration of souls. Who was He, then?

Before that question is answered, there's a very important discovery I have made: God will let us believe whatever we need to believe in order to get us moving to the place of His purpose. Consider the authentic truths and lies that have been passed down the last two thousand years! Because there are no dead ends in God to the sincere believer, we know all things do work together for good to them that love God. (See Romans 8:28.) Just remember, God has a way of redeeming even the things we don't understand. He moves whether we are on the same frequency with Him or not. The Kingdom of God involves movement. We're moving from spiritual adolescence to spiritual maturity, from the Feast of Pentecost to the Feast of Tabernacles, from anointing to glory. Whatever the setting, everything in the environment networks toward a shift of perception. God is dedicated to advancing His Kingdom.

When Peter said, "You are the Christ," he set the stage for further revelation from Jesus. Of course, Christ knew flesh and blood and the carnal realm had not given this inspiration to oft-fleshly Peter. What he was saying was supernatural revelation directly flowing as a pure, death-free stream from the throne of God. The Father in Heaven had rolled the curtains back and lifted the veil from Peter's mind. Revelation is about unveiling what is veiled, disclosing the things closed, and unfolding what is folded. It delivers us from the spirit of what everyone else is saying in igno-rance. Revelation is always an adjustment to the mediocre, vague, and nonspecific way we thought up to that point.

The Christ is the reason for the Church; therefore, the Church must be Christ-centered. The spiritual knowledge Peter received from the Father set the tone and foundation for everything that was to follow. By speaking the unadul-terated truth concerning the Christ, he created an opportu-nity to frame that truth in his sphere of influence. Allow me to explain. Nothing on Earth happens until someone speaks! Our words will either help establish the present reality of Christ and the Church or they will be idle words. God is a creative thinker and master craftsman extraordinaire. Although these facts are undeniably true, nothing happened in creation until He spoke. Out of that powerful display of divine activity, a law arises: Whatever God said, God saw! Since we are created in His image, the same law applies to us: We will have whatever we say.

What is God's idea of the word *church*? A brief study of the Greek word translated "church" will clarify the matter.

Inherently, God's idea of church is in the definition of the word and the law of first use. Popular traditions have confused the word in the hearing of modern man. We have ascribed this word primarily to buildings (such as "the Church house"), a denominational group or para-church organization ("the Pentecostal Church"), and even mid-week and weekend gatherings ("Did you go to church?").[3] In the peculiar sense of the word, not any of these concepts are biblically sound. From the Day of Pentecost onward, the New Testament is replete with God's idea of Church.

Church comes from the Greek word *ekklesia*, which was a political assembly. It evolved to be an official gathering of the full citizens of a Greek city-state, who were called together to make political and judicial judgments.[4] The witty, heady Greeks did not use *ekklesia* to mean religious gatherings.

When Jesus used this term, it was flavored with revolutionary connotations. The Church has been and always will be a politically incorrect, alternate society. It is asinine to think the world system will ever totally welcome and embrace the inalienable rights of the Church. Our right to exist is based upon the irrevocable statement of Jesus, "I will build My Church." The Church exists as a divine contradiction in the midst of an anti-God, antichrist culture. It is His gathering—not Caesar or Herod's. There is nothing political or religious about the Church in terms of human politics. She is relational and ministry-oriented. Herein lies the reason for Christ wrestling His Church out of the hands of carnal, covetous, and corrupt men today. They have turned His Church into a bastion of iniquity and a den of clever, conniving showmen, with performance—not servant power—as the *modus operandi*. An example of this is the unscrupulous, covetous practices of men with money. Also, some men abuse authority through sexual misconduct with their spiritual children. These things should not happen!

By not choosing the word *synagogue* and using the term *church*, Jesus was breaking from His Jewish roots. Out of their dispersion into Babylonian captivity came the synagogue concept. Sabbath meetings were held in the synagogue, which had come to symbolize the Jewish faith to the Greek world. God was developing "a new wineskin." When Jesus used *ekklesia*, in one sense it was a redemption of the word and, therefore, reset its emphasis in the minds of His disciples.

The etymology of *ekklesia* compounds two Greek words, *ek* (out) and *kaleo* (to call), essentially meaning a called-out assembly.[5] Church happens when people are called out and summoned for a destiny together. People who hear the voice of Jesus are called out into a unique, joined-together society. The cultural application of this calling is a new society. People would form a community and make a commitment to the radical lifestyle of Jesus and His Kingdom expressed in God's Word. It is a covenant to Jesus, not preacher and priests, that makes the Church different.

Ekklesia appears three times in the Gospels: once in Matthew 16:18 (the universal Church) and twice in Matthew 17:18 (the local church). A local church is a group of believers who gather under the auspices of the Holy Spirit and the Lordship of Jesus Christ to reinforce a vision and set of convictions about Him. The Church is universal to the degree that it is the assemblage of all the communities and regions of the Earth, including those precious saints in the Heavens. In applying this thought, the apostles, elders, and the community in the Acts and the Epistles set forth our usage of *Church* today.

Through all of our divisions and schemes, we have complicated something Christ made simple. Basically the Church is the ratifying of a corporate community. Ideas like corporation and board meetings were foreign to the first-century Christian because they were busy staying alive and living out the principles Jesus taught them. Judaism and Rome hated them with perfect hatred. There was no way Caesar or Herod would have granted them an exemption from state taxation. The more standard terminology of the relationship between Jesus and the Church are found in words like *father* and *sons*, *brothers* and *sisters*, *body* and *workmanship*, *family* and *friends*, *house* and *temple*, and *bridegroom* and *bride*. These are all relational, organic terms, which foster a family and community consciousness.

One of the great metaphors describing the Church in the New Testament is "the whole family!" (See Ephesians 3:14-15.) This is the fifth of seven word pictures Paul gives of the Church in Ephesians, making it one of the central ones. A commonly accepted definition for family would be a fundamental social group consisting of a man and woman and their offspring or all the members of a household living under the same roof. The extended family would be a group of people sharing a common ancestry and a distinguished lineage. When Paul uses the concept, "the whole family," it should be very apparent he's speaking of the entire extended family as members of God's *household*. (See Ephesians 2:19.)

If we play on words, *the whole family* is *whole*, not broken and dysfunctional. From Heaven's perspective, this is always the case. However, on Earth we tend to tear apart the family through selfish, individually motivated desires. Some person or group will arise with ambitions inconsistent with the purposes of God. Things on the surface appear to be intact; nevertheless, underneath there is much that needs repair. Webster defines *dysfunction* as "abnormal, impaired, or incomplete functioning, as of a body organ or part."[6] Because the Church is a living organism, we must come to grips with divine order and desire, or we will be no different from many of the modern families sociologists describe as dysfunctional. This problem is so epidemic in modern society that entire fields of scholastic discipline have been given to study its fallout.

Having been reared with six siblings, I thoroughly understand many of the concepts the Bible espouses as principles of family life. Although we had our share of challenges, as all families do, we learned many vital lessons necessary to be functional adults. A list of some of those principles is as follows:

157

1. We had a father from whom the family derived its name. This not only enabled us to focus upon our immediate father, but also to pay attention to the forefather who is the origin of the family identity. As children of God, we all have the same genetic code and blood, which makes us brethren with the same destiny. On the natural plane we are Abraham's seed (see Gal. 3:29); and in the spiritual realm we are all sons of God (see Jn. 1:11-13).

2. Because my parents were married, which is the most basic relationship of stable society, our home was one of *nurture* and *admonition*, as described in Ephesians 6:4. Our parents tenderly trained each of us without exasperating us. We knew that the family was central in communicating faith, purpose, and a sense of destiny to the children. Also, we came to understand that marriage is honorable in all because it represents the highest ideal of covenant-keeping.

3. By living in the same household, we came to appreciate the deep sense of family, to mutually respect one another, and to live and love together as brothers and sisters. This was the ideal context for building personal relationships. The New Testament pays much attention to quality relationships in families. (See Ephesians 5:22–6:9; Colossians 3:12-24; First Peter 3:1-7; Romans 12:9-16; First Timothy 5.)

4. Although all of my siblings are adults and some of us live many miles apart, we still share a deep sense of comradeship. We take care of one another, show deep affection for one another, spend pleasurable time together when we can, and share distinct responsibilities when we must. (See Acts 2:42-46; James 2:15-16; Romans 16:16; First Corinthians 16:20; Hebrews 10:24-25; First Timothy 5; Titus 2:1-10).

5. The family has the principle of multiplicity and exponential growth locked into its seed. Children of a family will ultimately reproduce themselves, therefore

extending the family. This is equally true concerning the Church. As the Body of Christ, our purpose is to grow up into the Head: a vertical growth, mainly consisting of the character and nature of Christ. Conversely, as the family we grow up and grow out. It is horizontal growth as well as begetting new members into the family. (See Acts 2:41; 4:4; 5:14; 6:1; 9:31; 16:5.)

Even in a day and age when we are misguided somewhat by numbers and quantity, the Church still may encompass any number of believers, from two or three to literally thousands. Unfortunately the real question remains, "Are they gathered and divinely assembled under the headship of Jesus Christ?" In its embryonic state, the Church mainly gathered in small groups in houses. (See Romans 16:5.) There were citywide churches as well, consisting of all believers in large cities. (See Acts 11:22; 13:1; First Corinthians 1:2.) A large geographical region, such as Asia Minor, would include more than one church. (See First Corinthians 16:1,19.) Wherever the word *Church* is used, regardless of whether it has small community, citywide, or regional connotations, we are to discern our corporate identity and edify one another as we function.

Within this context, the twenty-first century Church must find her niche. Are we going to re-envision what Christ had in mind when He first uttered the word Church, or not? Many wonderful volumes have been written about the Church, from house groups to large apostolic structures, and many more will follow as we decode the present emphasis of the Holy Spirit. Yet, when we hear the word *Church*, we all need to clear our heads of the foggy conditions in which our Western culture and religious, theological debates have left us. Our tangents and immovable positions have left the Church with many "crippling issues." Purity of definition leaves us no choice but to understand that Church is about believers, as in all of them, functioning in community. It is not hierarchical orders, buildings, denominations, Sunday meetings, or anything else. Just people—people in divine order. Not a single one of us can go to church—*we are church!*

Jesus, the greatest Church-builder, never built a building, established a building fund budget, or invested multi-millions of dollars in property. He built and empowered people, and that's the plain truth! He gave them divine strategy (a plan of the Father's purpose), a divine tactic (arrangement of their forces), and divine mobilization (places the forces before the enemy in divine order). God the Father has work that must be finished! In the initial stages of the New Testament Church, people of initiative and enterprising spirits had to lead. People of initiative always possess drive, determination, and desire. As Kingdom enterprisers, they are bold, daring, and have the ability to think outside of the current wineskin without being urged. Peter and all the apostles fit this description. When Jesus chose the apostles after praying all night, He knew He had chosen the right group—even if one was a devil. An honest appraisal of what these men accomplished proved Jesus right.

Apostolic Source

Jesus is the apostolic source of the Church. The writer of the Book of the Hebrews says, "Consider the Apostle and High Priest of our confession, Christ Jesus" (Heb. 3:1b). No other person may call themselves the apostle except Jesus. Everyone else falls into the category of "some apostles" in Ephesians 4:11. The Church finds her origin in Him. The gaping hole in His side was the birthing matrix for the Church to come out of Him just as the first woman was built from materials out of the side of the man. We are bone of His bone and flesh of His flesh.

Some Christians clamor to be known as apostles because they are often title-conscious and character-thin. Little do they realize that this ministry function (apostles) is groomed on the anvil of suffering. (See Second Corinthians 11:22-28.) For some reason they think it gives them a higher rank and status in the religious pecking order, a higher pedigree. Actually, it is just the opposite in the Kingdom of God. The apostles are set forth as last in the program and occupy a place in the foundation of the building. (See First Corinthians 4:9; Ephesians 2:20.) This projects them as being over no one, under everyone, and last in line. Once again, correction is needed in the modern Western Church. We have pandered with so many Babylonian concepts that our perspectives are way off.

At this point, someone may ask, "Why are apostles mentioned first, then, in First Corinthians 12:28?" *First* is the Greek word *proton*, signifying "firstly (in time, place, order, or importance):—before, at the beginning."[7] It is an adverb modifying the action of the apostolic ministry, not the apostolic person. The idea dons breakthrough potential and not hierarchical importance. Apostles are the first to tread unbroken territory for the Kingdom of God. Metaphorically they are plows that break open the fallow ground of old and new regimes. Apostles are not more important than other charismatic gifts because all gifts are expressions of Christ's total ministry. Other ministry gifts of equal importance follow apostles once they have paved the way.

Since apostles are first, they absorb the most ridicule, catch the initial flack, and are possible candidates for torture or murder. Today, that means apostles are first on the hit list for accusation and character assassination. We are failing to understand that apostles are called to make full the sufferings of Jesus. Men and women in the suffering Church serve as an example for us in this. Most Western apostles are well protected behind the beautiful wall of human rights. For this I am grateful. However, the same is not true for many apostles within the part of the world known as the 10/40 window. These firebrands of faith are to be interceded for and held in the highest regard. They are suffering miserably under oppressive religious or atheistic regimes because they dare love Jesus.

161

Jesus chooses "some" men and women to serve as representative apostolic source ministries in the Church. Peter, who received the revelation of Christ, became such an example. He was a channel of release for the desire of Heaven to make contact with the Earth. Note the different times Peter spoke or acted as the representative apostle:

- Peter received the revelation and the keys to the Kingdom. (See Matthew 16:17-19.)
- Peter stood in the midst of the disciples and spoke. (See Acts 1:15.)
- Peter stood with the other 11 apostles, raised his voice, and spoke. (See Acts 2:14.)
- Peter boldly spoke to rulers, elders, and former sorcerers as a representative apostle. (See Acts 4:8; 5:29; 8:20.)
- Peter spoke apostolic judgments on the treachery of Ananias and Sapphira. (See Acts 5:1-11.)
- Peter was the first recorded apostle to raise the dead. (See Acts 9:36-43.)
- Peter received the vision concerning the next major wave of the Holy Spirit to keep the Church current and on the cutting edge of God's activity. (See Acts 10:9-16,34-44.)
- God worked in Peter the apostleship to the circumcised. (See Galatians 2:8.)

Jesus said to Peter, the representative apostle,

And I will give you the keys of the kingdom of heaven, and whatever you bind on earth will be bound in heaven, and whatever you loose on earth will be loosed in heaven. Matthew 16:19

At this point we must understand that the Kingdom is the big picture; the Church is a smaller picture. It is as though the Church, moving in authority, is a subset of the whole set called the Kingdom of God. Israel was known as the Church in the wilderness (see Acts 7:38) and purposed to be a *Kingdom of priests* (see Ex. 19:6). The New Testament Church is a Kingdom embassy, which is the extension of God's rule or domain in the Earth. God's sovereign right to govern and His governmental order is revealed through His Church. (See Romans 4:17; First Corinthians 4:20; Revelation 11:15.) It is equally important to remember that Jesus spoke more often about the Kingdom than He did about the Church. Peter, and any other representative apostle, could only speak what Heaven had already determined.

The basis of all delegated authority is found in this statement: "I will give you the keys of the kingdom of heaven" (Mt. 16:19). Government in the Kingdom of God is administered by the principle of delegated authority, which is to be entrusted with Christ's authority. Apostles, along with the other ministries, are sent to the Church as Christ's delegates. Acceptance of the delegate meant acceptance of the one who sent the delegate. A true New Testament ministry always comes to God's people *under authority* and not with the egotistical attitude that they are *the authority*.

All authority and power are given for service; otherwise, they become a means of fear, intimidation, and manipulation. The rabbis had abused authority. Jesus was officially terminating the rabbis' claim to the powers of "binding and loosing" and "prohibiting and permitting." Also, considering the usage of these words in other texts, these were the powers of forgiving or retaining sin. (See Matthew 18:18; John 20:22-23.) Such a statement would declare a thing lawful or unlawful.

As an occupational force the Church still has binding and loosing powers. We tolerate many adversarial assaults without exercising our rights of refusal. Before something or some charlatan devoid of character comes into a region and devastates it with ungodly and unscrupulous practices, the apostolic council of that region should either permit or prohibit him. Now, before you say, "That's too much control!" please listen:

> *For there are a lot of rebels out there, full of loose,*
> *confusing, and deceiving talk. Those who were brought*

163

up religious and ought to know better are the worst. They've got to be shut up. They're disrupting entire families with their teaching, and all for the sake of a fast buck. Titus 1:10-11 TM

But there were also lying prophets among the people then, just as there will be lying religious teachers among you. They'll smuggle in destructive divisions, pitting you against each other—biting the hand of the One who gave them a chance to have their lives back! They put themselves on a fast downhill slide to destruction, but not before they recruit a crowd of mixed-up followers who can't tell right from wrong.

2 Peter 2:1-2 TM

Many broken lives would be spared irreparable damage if this checks-and-balance system operated. In the beginning days of the Church, the Church did not officially receive a ministry gift unless there was an accompanying letter of commendation. (See Second Corinthians. 3:1.)

I do, however, understand that in past times clergymen have stood in the gate of the city and repressed the move of God because of fear. As clarions of one realm of truth, they have disregarded and even anathematized other truths. This shouldn't cause us to cast all caution to the wind and receive anything just because it names the name of Jesus and appeals charismatically. Apostles will always hammer out truth and the authenticity of any move of God. They stand in a city or region to represent Jesus, the apostolic source of the Church. With legislative and judicial powers, apostles help to keep the Church on the right foundation.

Finally, as a representative apostolic source, there are very important principles to regard. One is in the exercise of meekness and temperance with your speech. It is not proper to blurt everything one knows. An over-inflated ego may release information much before God intends for it to be released. Believe me, God is not impressed with such impetuosity! Meekness is an even-tempered spirit that is neither elated nor cast down, simply because it is not occupied with self at all. A meek man or woman has nothing to prove—no reason to impress anybody. They are the complete opposite of self-assertiveness and self-interest.

There are certain revelations unlawful to tell until we receive permission from the Holy Spirit to release what we have seen. In doing so, we prove ourselves trustworthy and therefore become approved of God. (See Second Corinthians 12:1-7; Galatians 1:11-12; Ephesians 3:1-5.) In His discourse with the apostles, Jesus said: "Tell no man I am the Messiah!" They were to ponder this newfound information quietly. The season for His full manifestation was not yet come. Jesus was unwilling to provoke further systematic malice or Roman ire by permitting His disciples to publish what they knew out of season. This information was to be held under tight wraps until after His passion and subsequent resurrection. After the resurrection and ascension, this truth would be set forth in the clearest sublimity, beyond the power of any contradiction.

TRANSITION'S TRIUMPH

The Cross is the means of both transition and triumph. After the revelation that Jesus was the Christ, the Scripture says, "From that time Jesus began to show His disciples that He must go to Jerusalem, and suffer many things from the elders and chief priests and scribes, and be killed, and be raised the third day" (Mt. 16:21).

"From that time" is a prepositional phrase indicating transition. The small band of disciples is clearly now in transition, just as the modern Church has been for the last decade or more. Their education required perceiving some alternative concepts they were basically unwilling to accept.

They believe that the long-awaited, revealed Messiah, Jesus, would surely mobilize Israel and overthrow Roman tyranny. The disciples were guilty of the same thing that we are at times; they failed to allow the Lord to interpret His own expectation. Immediately Peter was cast into the uncomfortable position of seeking control and at the same time being in opposition to the will of God. Surely, if he had revelation concerning the Christ, he was qualified to counsel Jesus. He was now attempting to contradict the predetermined will of God.

Webster defines *contradiction* as "a statement in opposition to another; denial; it is a condition in which things tend to be contrary to each other; inconsistency, discrepancy."[8] The Greek word translated "contradiction" in Hebrews 7:7; 12:3 is antilogia. This stems from two word parts: *anti* (against) and *logos* (word).[9] The simple definition would be to oppose the Word. *Antilogia*, then, is anything or anyone that is inconsistent with the Word of God and seeks to impose their personal persuasions on that which is divine. That, in itself, produces a discrepancy.

Joseph and David, two "men of destiny," were exposed to experiences inconsistent with the prophetic word over their lives. They each received a word concerning their destinies and subsequently entered into a season of unsolicited new dealings. (See Psalm 105:17-22; Psalm 57.) For 13 years every inch of their souls was tried. The eternal viewpoint was to bring them to pure gold. The fires of trial and testing burned profusely until God's expected end was achieved.

> *But He knows the way I take; when He has tested me, I shall come forth as gold.* Job 23:10

The purpose of contradiction is to shake us to our core. It's the startling reality that our destiny is etched into the wooden fibers of the cross. God will always announce the end from the beginning and then march us back to the beginning to walk us through the process firsthand. There is no way to dodge this! Either we will submit to the will of God or internal strife will besiege us. And if it does, strife manifests itself as offense because of a failure to maintain proper perspective concerning the Word of His purpose. The deceiver will make us think either God lied or the prophet did.

That spiritual door which opened inside Peter long enough to receive and process the revelation of the Messiah momentarily closed. He was colored by offense with the last word from Heaven. His humanity, just as ours, wanted to tame, train, box up, and frame the revelation. Because he could not do this, he became frightened and trapped by the words of Jesus and bit the bait of offense. The Greek word for offense is *skandalon*. Once again, one should immediately see the English word *scandal*. A scandal is generally someone whose conduct causes disgrace or shame. It is actually the middle ground to either grow spiritually or circulate in old behavior. Accepting the rebuke of Jesus produces growth; rejecting it causes further circulation into selfishness.

There are great stewardship requirements when one has the most current, cutting-edge message of the day. Apostles and prophets are called to steward the present emphasis of God and maintain its sacredness. (See First Corinthians 4:1.) Peter had the new message; however, he did not have the proper wineskin or mentality with which to process what he was receiving. God has been prophetically speaking concerning the Feast of Tabernacles for the last 50 years or more. Unfortunately the Church was not unified and ready to process what He was saying. Thus, the Cross is the means of transition.

The Word of the Lord exposed and crossed Peter's carnality. Our carnalities and discrepancies are under the same brutal edge of a flaming sword. In each case, Peter and we are pressed to behold what is ordinarily veiled: We are grossly insecure, and always given to self-preservation. Our concepts must be transformed in order to agree with His. Also, our mental condition is our spiritual position. "For as he thinks in his heart, so is he" (Prov. 23:7).

Jesus was giving the key to release this Christ of God in order that the entire Earth might be blessed and benefit from His presence. The man from Galilee was limited to one body, whereas the Christ of God could vigorously inhabit many at once. The cross would pierce His human

167

shell, therefore inaugurating a new and living way into the Spirit. (See Hebrews 10:20.) It took a body of life to reform the deformed generational cycle of the body of death. God created a man of high estate (a living being), and Adam made him carnal, and of a low estate (a body of death)—far beneath the original intention. The cruel cross broke the outer shell, the greedy grave received the seed for planting, and the glorious resurrection permitted the new economy of life to emerge. (See John 12:23-26.) The same generational cycle would have continued indefinitely until someone who was supernaturally empowered invaded and reversed it.

This same principle is very evident also in the early days of the sixteenth century Protestant Reformation. Romanism had created an unhealthy cycle of religious control and death. Europe as a whole was no longer ethereal and spiritually focused. Hedonism, a belief that the purpose of life is pleasure—both sensual and intellectual—was quickly becoming the dominant philosophy. Secular scholars were returning to the ideals of pagan antiquity. Life was glorified in the "here and now" and essentially indifferent to spiritual claims. Mankind was no longer viewed as depraved but deemed inherently good. Powerful individualism and independence created an intense desire and taste for many previously forbidden appetites by Middle-Age repulsion.

It was within this same time frame that God stirred Martin Luther, the German reformer, to action. He inadvertently began a second major movement (the Renaissance had already begun in the 1300s and 1400s). According to history, Luther, a priest at the University of Wittenberg, went on a mission to Rome in 1510 in the interest of the Augustinian Order, of which he was a member. With preconceptions that Rome truly was the holy city and the supreme seat of holiness, and the pope was the vicar of Christ, his convictions were about to be shockingly reversed. He was extremely shell-shocked by the spiritual laxity and degeneration in high places. Provoked to action, Luther's spiritual quest intensified. The wicked deeds of dignitaries were disappointing and beyond his comprehension.

What made Luther passionately revolt and risk his life to tackle uncharted waters? From about 1516 Luther began to protest the idea of indulgences (certificates to remit sins) preached by John Tetzel. Tetzel preached and promoted this idea to create an influx of money into the Roman Catholic treasury. It was a diabolical system attaching money rather than blood to God's forgiveness. Obliged to do something to resist this ungodly teaching and system of profiteering, Luther protested. Thus the beginnings of the formal ideology called "Protestantism."

October 31, 1517, Luther posted his historical 95 Theses, stating the evils of indulgences. The man whom God had dealt with privately, crafted in obscurity, had now come into the open. He must stand upon the foundations of passion and knowledge. He became the living epistle of the Lord's zeal along with the Lord's Word. A revolution had begun. Like an arrow launched from a bowstring under intense pressure, the nailing of the Theses signified the point of no return. It was to be a sound that changed everything. Not totally sure of the outcome, he was too convicted to stop now. The fuel for this was in the shed blood of the saints from the pre-Reformation days mingled with the burnt offerings of their bodies. The voice of their blood compares to faithful Abel's: Whereas Abel's cried revenge, theirs cried *reformation*!

PREVAILING TRANSITION

Martin Luther had to embrace the practicality of the Cross in order to do what he did. Transition prevails when we, by the medium of the Cross, say *yes* to the will of God. This should be a daily proclamation and procedure. As wandering Israel left pillaged, battered Egypt, an aerial view of them encamped would reveal the Cross. Once the Tabernacle was erected, the furniture was arranged in the form of a cross. Their entire lives, socially and religiously, revolved around the Cross. Thus, there is a cross within a cross, which constitutes double-crossed. This is not the humanistic, secular meaning of double-crossed, which is "betrayal."

It seems that God the Father had double-crossed them in not fully exposing His plan to purge their selfishness and bitterness before they could enter the Promised Land. They were sifted of the carnal, the rebellious, the complainers, the idolaters, and the sexually immoral. God instituted ordinances of purification that involved various washings and burnt sacrifices. Fire and water—two powerful cleansing agents—are the spiritual application of double-crossed. He had spoken profound, exceptional words of value concerning their destiny, but very few in regards to the process of their purity. God triumphantly moved them from vagabonds to peculiar people, a kingdom of priests ready to occupy their destiny through the Cross.

The personal application of this triumphant transition lies in how we process the words of Jesus: "If anyone desires to come after Me, let him deny himself, and take up his cross, and follow Me" (Mt. 16:24).

This was so important that each of the synoptic gospel writers, Matthew, Mark, and Luke, mentions this thought. Denying generally means to abjure and to utterly deny as having no connections with one's desires. Every person preparing to embrace the new day in God must determine what could capture their affections more than God. Self-denial strengthens anyone to effectively take up the cross, without murmuring and disputation. Pure individuality is dealt a deathblow, and we are energized for corporate matriculation.

Remember, it is your personal cross, not His eternal or historical Cross. This verse is a conditional invitation because everyone will not choose this course. Too many believers desire a cross-less life today. Apart from the cross, there is no way to complete the process of our change. However, to those who do, the high calling of God in Christ Jesus awaits them. One cannot effectively move to something new until there's a willingness to divest the old, even if it means *you*.

God's idea of Church is people transformed by the power of the Holy Spirit as He works through the cross in their lives with a Kingdom agenda. The end result is manifesting the life of King Jesus by becoming His visible illumination. The Church is His living epistle, His lively stones, and His house in the Earth. Human beings are still saying, "Sir, we wish to see Jesus" (Jn. 12:21). Jesus is now seen and known through His Church, which is His Body. When Saul, later Paul, was a terrorist ambushing believers, little did he know this was Jesus He was persecuting. (See Acts 9:4-5.) The point is simple: Jesus is not someone other than His Body, of which He happens to be the Head.

I realize the same man who left will return on God's appointed day; however, for now we must see him in His Body. It is only the lawless antichrist spirit that refuses to see Him within His Body. A transformed Paul, in speaking of the interdependence of the Body of Christ, said, "For as the body is one and has many members, but all the members of that one body, being many, are one body, so also is Christ" (1 Cor. 12:12).

Christ is one Body, and the head of that Body is Jesus.

Our human body is made up of trillions of cells, all working together as tissues, organs, and systems for the good of the body. No one cell can get blown up into self-importance and become isolationist.

> *The way God designed our bodies is a model for understanding our lives together as a Church: every part dependent on every other part, the parts we mention and the parts we don't, the parts we see and the parts we don't. If one part hurts, every other part is involved in the hurt, and in the healing. If one part flourishes, every part enters into the exuberance.*
>
> *You are Christ's body—that's who you are! You must never forget this. Only as you accept your part of that body does your "part" mean anything.*
>
> 1 Corinthians 12:24-27 TM

ENDNOTES

1. Virginia Ely, *I Quote* (New York: George W. Stewart, Publisher, Inc., 1947), 73.

2. Adapted from Alfred Edersheim, *The Life and Times of Jesus the Messiah*, Vol. 2, Book 3 (Peabody, MA: Hendrickson Publishers, 1993), 74.

3. Adapted from Lawrence O. Richards, *Expository Dictionary of Bible Words* (Grand Rapids, MI: Zondervan Publishing House, 1991), 164.

4. Ibid.

5. James Strong, "Greek Dictionary of the New Testament," *The New Strong's Complete Dictionary of Bible Words* (Nashville: Thomas Nelson Publishers, 1996), #1577, #1537, #2564.

6. *Webster's New World College Dictionary, Third Edition*, Victoria Neufeldt, ed. (New York: Simon & Schuster, Inc., 1997), 424.

7. Strong, "Greek Dictionary of the New Testament," #4412.

8. *Webster's*, 302.

9. Strong, "Greek Dictionary of the New Testament," #485, #473, #3004.

Also by
STEPHEN EVERETT

THE MYSTERY OF MELCHISEDEC

Just who is this mysterious man who appears only once in the Old Testament? Does he represent a revelation of Christ yet to unfold in the Church? Does he possibly personify a new administration in God, untarnished by almost 2,000 years of Church strife, wars, and traditions? The message in this book answers with clarity these questions and more.

ISBN: 1-56043-036-2

Additional copies of this book and other book titles from DESTINY IMAGE are available at your local bookstore.

For a complete list of our titles, visit us at www.destinyimage.com Send a request for a catalog to:

Destiny Image® Publishers, Inc.

P.O. Box 310
Shippensburg, PA 17257-0310

"Speaking to the Purposes of God for This Generation and for the Generations to Come"